How to Grow
Plants
for Free

RHS How to Grow Plants for Free

Author: Simon Akeroyd

First published in Great Britain in 2023 by Mitchell Beazley, a division of Octopus Publishing Group Ltd
Carmelite House, 50 Victoria Embankment, London EC4Y 0DZ
www.octopusbooks.co.uk

An Hachette UK Company
www.hachette.co.uk

Published in association with the Royal Horticultural Society

ISBN: 978-1-78472-891-5

A CIP record of this book is available from the British Library

Printed and bound in China

Conceived, designed and produced by The Bright Press
an imprint of The Quarto Group
1 Triptych Place, London
SE1 9SH, United Kingdom
T (0) 20 7700 6700
www.quarto.com

Publisher: James Evans
Art Director: James Lawrence
Editorial Director: Isheeta Mustafi
Managing Editor: Jacqui Sayers
Senior Editor: Caroline Elliker
Project Editor: Katie Crous
Editorial Assistant, Octopus: Jeannie Stanley
Design: JC Lanaway
Cover Design: Emily Nazer
Illustrations: John Woodcock

Mitchell Beazley Publisher: Alison Starling
RHS Publisher: Helen Griffin
RHS Consultant Editor: Simon Maughan
RHS Head of Editorial: Tom Howard

The Royal Horticultural Society is the UK's leading gardening charity dedicated to advancing horticulture and promoting good gardening. Its charitable work includes providing expert advice and information, training the next generation of gardeners, creating hands-on opportunities for children to grow plants and conducting research into plants, pests and environmental issues affecting gardeners.
For more information visit www.rhs.org.uk or call 0845 130 4646.

 **RHS**

How to Grow
Plants
for Free

CREATING NEW PLANTS FROM
CUTTINGS, SEEDS AND MORE

SIMON AKEROYD

MITCHELL BEAZLEY

Contents

Chapter 4

Chapter 5

Chapter 6

INTRODUCTION

Filling a house and/or garden full of plants that you have grown yourself is one of the most rewarding things you can do in the world of gardening. It is incredibly satisfying to nurture a new plant from its conception to maturity. Yet any cursory glance online or at a garden centre will confirm that new plants can be costly. So here is the solution: *How to Grow Plants for Free* shows you how to grow, nurture and enjoy plants that have cost you next to nothing.

Of course, it's not just about saving money. It's also about conserving varieties in your garden that might not be available commercially anymore. Knowing how to collect seeds and take cuttings will help keep the variety alive.

Once you have gained the knowledge and skills to propagate plants, you can choose whatever plants you fancy, be it garden-centre varieties or those found in the local countryside. Your friends' and family's gardens will become your 'free shop', where you can pick and choose favourites to grace your own garden.

A word of warning, though. The thrill, delight and anticipation of starting to grow your own plants for free can become addictive. Windowsills, coffee tables, porches and any other surfaces may overflow with seed trays, cuttings and propagators. Outside, pots, containers and flowerbeds will be bursting with beautiful free plants. You may want to share this possible surplus, through gifts, selling or swapping. And joining a gardening club or allotment could open up a whole new network, or even new friendships.

This book explains everything there is to know about how to propagate a plant for free, from how to collect and sow seed, to how to divide up roots and split plants up into yet more horticultural freebies. There is guidance on taking hardwood, softwood, leaf and root cuttings, along with plant profiles dotted throughout, featuring beautiful, individual plants that are easy to propagate from.

No longer will you find yourself gazing at other people's flourishing plants, wondering how to get your hands on something similar. With a bit of knowledge and patience, and a plant- or land-owner's permission, almost all the plants you see can be yours.

HOW TO USE THIS BOOK

Whether it's with seeds, cuttings or by division, this book will show you everything you need to know about filling your garden full of beautiful, free plants.

CHAPTER 1

Introduces the science behind propagation, with tips on observing and helping out our natural environment. Includes a list of tools and equipment, as well as information on compost types. Explains the best places to grow your plants, including step-by-step guides to using recycled materials for propagators and pots.

CHAPTER 2

Looks at how to divide plants – possibly the easiest way to propagate. Explains the different methods to split plants and create lots of free ones to either replant or give away.

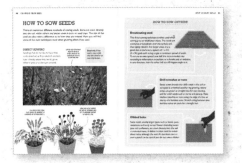

CHAPTER 3

A primer on the magic of growing from seed, with information on how to harvest and store seeds, as well as different techniques of sowing and growing them.

CHAPTER 4

Cuttings can get you the exact copy of your favourite plants. Includes information on stem cuttings: hardwood, semi-ripe and softwood; as well as steps on how to take leaf and root cuttings.

CHAPTER 5

Shows how to grow your favourite houseplants so that you never run out of exciting interior floral or foliage displays. Explains how to propagate using leaf cuttings, stem cuttings in water, offshoots and much more.

CHAPTER 6

Gives the lowdown on growing free plants from the huge range found on supermarket shelves, from sprouting vegetable scraps to growing seeds from melons and apple pips.

PLANT PROFILES

In Chapters 2 to 6, individual plant profiles offer ideas and inspiration, including different varieties to choose to propagate, with notes on how to care for them once they are growing and how to harvest any fruits of your labour.

At the back you will find a botanical glossary illustrating the various plant parts and the different ways they can grow. This is useful to know when looking to propagate from them. There is also a standard glossary explaining some of the terminology used in the world of gardening.

CHAPTER 1

GETTING STARTED

The world of plant propagation is a fascinating one. There are lots of exciting techniques to learn and, once mastered, you will be able to produce as many free plants as you have room for.

How to Grow Plants for Free is a gentle introduction to the basics of plant propagation, starting with how plants grow from seeds and cuttings, both in the wild and with a gardener's help. From there, we look at how plants pollinate through to what they need to flourish, from using nature as a template to choosing compost and soil types. There's a handy list of inexpensive or freely available equipment as well as information on finding – and even making – the perfect plant home, be it a greenhouse, cold frame or simple pots.

Be sure to also check the illustrated glossary at the back of the book (pages 134–36), which explains some of the terminology you may come across when propagating plants, showing the various parts of a plant essential for successfully growing new ones.

This chapter is the beginning of your exciting journey into the world of plant propagation and discovering how to produce plants for free.

MAKING BABY PLANTS

There are plenty of occasions outside where you will see plants doing it for themselves without any intervention from us. In fact, being able to propagate plants successfully depends not only on understanding a plant's life cycle but also on closely observing how they reproduce in nature. The two most common techniques of reproducing a plant is sexually, with seed, or vegetatively, with cuttings. In most instances, this is by pollination, which produces seeds, and we will start there.

POLLINATION

For a seed to germinate, a female flower needs to receive pollen and be fertilised. Pollen, a fine powdery substance, is produced in sacs inside the male parts of a flower known as the anthers. Together with the filament, this part of the male flower is known as the stamen.

Although some plants are self-fertile, producing seed themselves without the assistance of other nearby plants, most need pollen from the anthers of another plant, often spread by an insect such as a bee or beetle entering the flower, brushing against the anthers as it forages for pollen and nectar, then knocking pollen onto another plant's female reproductive organs, known as the stigma.

The stigma, style and ovary are collectively known as the carpel and are the female part of the flower. When the pollen is transferred to the stigma and moves down the style and into the ovary, the seed becomes fertile and therefore ripe for reproduction.

The male and female parts of a typical flower are surrounded by petals.

The sepal is also part of the flower and is usually found at the base. Its role is to protect the flower bud as it emerges and then support the petals.

A helping hand

Encourage bees and other insects into the garden to pollinate flowers and produce seeds.

POLLEN IS COLLECTED FROM
THE STAMEN AND DEPOSITED
INTO THE STIGMA

MALE FLOWER

FEMALE FLOWER

For more information on botanical terms and plant anatomy, turn to pages 134–36.

Some plants such as the courgette produce separate male (above) and female (below) flowers.

Female flowers are often easy to recognise as they have a swollen ovary just below the petals.

FLOWER ATTRACTION

Plants have a few ingenious methods of attracting pollinators to help them with the transfer of pollen from the male to the female flower. The obvious one is to produce nectar that insects are drawn to and feed on. Some plants use bright colours to attract attention whilst others use a scent. Scents are not always sweet, either. The Titan arum (*Amorphophallus titanum*), or corpse flower, uses the aroma of rotting meat to attract flies. Some plants such as night-scented jasmine (*Cestrum nocturnum*) and evening primrose (*Oenothera biennis*) release their scent at night to attract moths as pollinators.

Using colour

To ensure seed ripens in the garden it is good to attract as many pollinators as possible. One of the ways this can be done is to have a range of different-coloured flowers. For example, bees are particularly attracted to violet–blue, because this can indicate high levels of nectar. Butterflies, on the other hand, prefer yellow, orange, pink and red.

Mimicking mates

Plants such as the bee orchid and the fly orchid attract pollinators by mimicking the shapes of potential 'mates'.

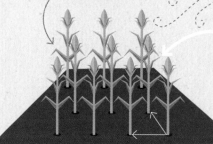

ARRANGING SWEETCORN PLANTS IN A GRID RATHER THAN IN A SINGLE ROW HELPS TO IMPROVE THE CHANCES OF SUCCESSFUL WIND POLLINATION.

PLANT IN A GRID OF THREE ROWS. LEAVE 30CM (12IN) BETWEEN PLANTS AND ROWS.

Wind pollination

Apart from attracting pollinators, there are other ingenious methods plants use to transfer pollen to female flowers. Plants such as sweetcorn and grapevines use wind as a natural vehicle to help blow pollen onto the flowers and become fertilised.

Grow a wide range of plants that will flower at different times of the year. Many bees are active for much of the year and need plants to forage on.

Keep a few 'weeds', such as dandelions and thistles, which bees love. Place dishes of water out in the garden (see page 19).

ONION

SUNFLOWER

SECRETS OF SEEDS

Seeds are amazing things. They are tiny, yet held within each one is an entire plant's DNA, hardwired to grow into a plant with roots, stems, leaves, flowers and sometimes to produce fruit, nuts or vegetables. Some will live for just a few months, whilst others such as an oak tree will live for hundreds of years.

ASSISTED POLLINATION

Some gardeners help with pollination of flowers to increase the amount of seed produced. This is often done on early-flowering plants where it is too cold for insects to be pollinating, or in greenhouses where creatures might not be able to access the flowers.

POLLINATION IS CARRIED OUT BY USING A SOFT PAINTBRUSH AND GENTLY STROKING THE INSIDE OF ONE PLANT THEN TRANSFERRING THE POLLEN TO ANOTHER FLOWER.

DID YOU KNOW? Not all seeds are tiny. The largest seed in the world is from the coco-de-mer palm (*Lodoicea maldivica*). Also known as the double coconut, it can weigh up to 25kg (55lb) and measure 30cm (12in) across.

LAVENDER

BEETROOT

SWEET PEA

DAHLIA

ECHINACEA

A PLANT'S LIFE CYCLE

In nature, most seeds will germinate if given the basic requirements for life: water, light, warmth and air. Gardeners can manipulate seeds to germinate by providing the same environment they need to grow.

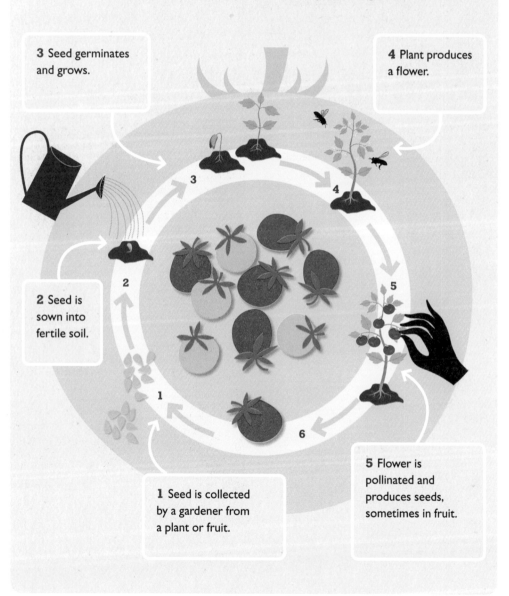

3 Seed germinates and grows.

4 Plant produces a flower.

2 Seed is sown into fertile soil.

1 Seed is collected by a gardener from a plant or fruit.

5 Flower is pollinated and produces seeds, sometimes in fruit.

NATURE KNOWS BEST

Plants are wonderful opportunists and will take any chance to spread themselves around. Observing them in the garden and wider nature can help us understand the various ways we can manipulate them to create new ones and enhance our natural environment. Probably the most obvious example of plants reproducing naturally is by looking at how plants, including many we might consider to be weeds, spread themselves in the garden.

SPREADING FAR AND WIDE

Like many wildflowers, dandelions produce seed heads that float in the wind and land elsewhere. This helps seeds to travel to new areas, expanding their gene pool as they spread further away from existing competition. Other plants such as yellow flag iris have seeds that can float on water to find new areas to germinate in. *Galium aparine* (sticky weed, also known as goose grass or cleavers) sticks onto the fur of animals such as foxes, badgers, dogs, or even human clothing, as they go past.

Other plants tempt pollinators – birds and other creatures – by covering their seeds in delicious fruit to be consumed and digested. Birds and other animals spread this seed through their droppings, ensuring that future seedlings get the best possible start as they land, covered in a dollop of natural fertiliser full of nutrients. In the same way, gardeners can mimic these conditions by feeding and fertilising plants as they grow.

We can emulate natural seed distribution by collecting seeds from our chosen plants and sowing them where we want them to grow.

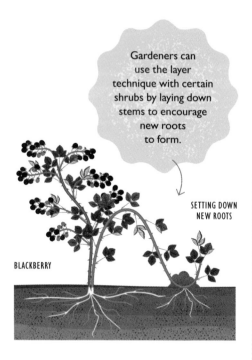

Gardeners can use the layer technique with certain shrubs by laying down stems to encourage new roots to form.

SETTING DOWN
NEW ROOTS

BLACKBERRY

ROOTING DOWN

Garden 'weeds' and wildflowers have an important role to play in encouraging pollinators into the garden, but some are highly adept at extending their family underground. Their exploratory roots spread through the ground as they multiply. If their roots are broken these parts regenerate into new plants. Gardeners can copy this ability by taking root cuttings of their favourite plants.

Whilst we all love the blackberry fruit produced from brambles, we also know they can run amok if left unattended. This is because they extend their family over and underground, through arching roots that take root at their tips, and 'layer' themselves by setting down new roots when stems come into contact with the soil.

MAKING A WILDLIFE-FRIENDLY GARDEN

It is estimated that 70 per cent of the world's food relies on bees for pollinating plants. They do this by inadvertently transferring pollen from one plant to another as they collect nectar and pollen. If you grow fruit or vegetables in your garden, your yields will be bigger if bees are visiting regularly. There are hundreds of types of bees and wasps, and they, along with other creatures such as flies, beetles, hoverflies and butterflies, have a role to play in pollination. Planting a wide range of different plants in the garden will encourage as many of them as possible to visit.

CREATE A BEE 'BAR'

Here's how to help bees and other flying insects survive summer:

- Select a wide-based shallow dish and position it in the garden.
- Place pebbles in the water so that insects can land on them and drink without drowning.
- Change the water regularly and keep it topped up to just below the height of the pebbles.

VEGETATIVE (ASEXUAL) PROPAGATION

Creating new plants from seed is known as sexual propagation. It requires a male and a female flower, and the new seedling will have unique characteristics, in the same way that we do not look identical to our parents. As we have seen with brambles, some plants have other non-sexual ways to regenerative themselves. This is called asexual or vegetative reproduction. It creates identical plants or clones, and because many plants can do it, it is a very useful way to create plants for free.

If you want to produce an identical plant to the one you already have, there is a way. Gardeners discovered centuries ago that it is easier to take a cutting from the plant. Similar to cloning, the process involves taking a section of the plant to replicate the parent plant.

PLANT CUTTINGS ARE MORE RELIABLE THAN SEEDS.

PLANTS GROWN FROM A SECTION OF THE PARENT PLANT.

Remarkably, almost all parts of a plant can be used to propagate from, although it will vary as to which sections are the most effective depending on the individual plant. It's best to research first as to what a specific plant's preference is regarding vegetative propagation.

ABOVE GROUND

Leaves

These can be used to propagate plants either as whole leaves or sections; it is a technique often used for houseplants (see page 116).

SEMI-RIPE
CUTTING

Stems

These can be taken as hardwood cuttings in winter, softwood cuttings from early spring, greenwood cuttings in early to midsummer and semi-ripe cuttings in mid- to late summer. Some stems growing close to the ground can be laid on the soil below it to stimulate more roots and eventually a new plant. This process is called layering (see opposite).

Aerial roots

Some plants produce aerial roots, which appear above ground. This is often the case with climbing or trailing plants, and certain houseplants. In some cases these sections of the plants can be removed and potted on to create new plants.

AERIAL
ROOTS

BELOW GROUND

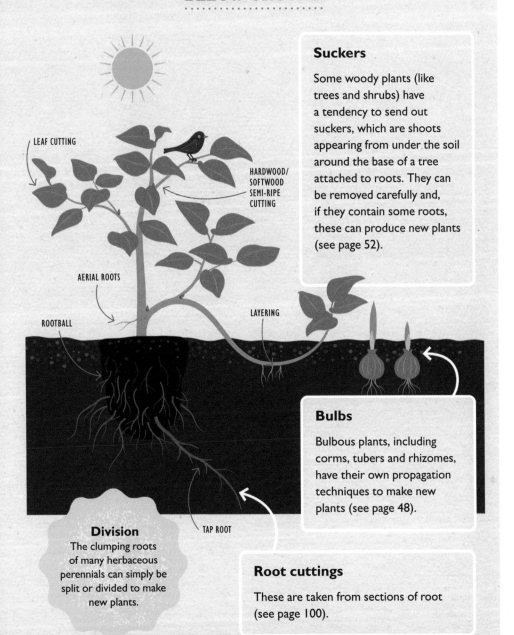

LEAF CUTTING

HARDWOOD/
SOFTWOOD
SEMI-RIPE
CUTTING

AERIAL ROOTS

ROOTBALL

LAYERING

TAP ROOT

Suckers

Some woody plants (like trees and shrubs) have a tendency to send out suckers, which are shoots appearing from under the soil around the base of a tree attached to roots. They can be removed carefully and, if they contain some roots, these can produce new plants (see page 52).

Bulbs

Bulbous plants, including corms, tubers and rhizomes, have their own propagation techniques to make new plants (see page 48).

Division

The clumping roots of many herbaceous perennials can simply be split or divided to make new plants.

Root cuttings

These are taken from sections of root (see page 100).

TOOLS AND EQUIPMENT

One of the key elements to growing plants successfully is having suitable tools and equipment. Happily, many of these are inexpensive or can be made for practically nothing. In fact, most propagation tools can easily be stored in cupboards or small outside sheds when they are not in use.

Generally, more expensive tools will be of a higher quality and last longer. It can be very pleasing to own nice tools; a good-quality pruning knife, for example, might be a treat to buy (or have as a present) and will be cherished for a lifetime. Always clean equipment and tools after use, putting them away properly to avoid breakages or damage.

DIBBERS CAN BE MADE OUT OF A SHARPENED PIECE OF WOOD, A PENCIL OR AN EMPTY BIRO.

MAKE PLANT LABELS FOR FREE USING OLD LOLLIPOP STICKS OR LONG STRIPS CUT FROM USED PLASTIC MILK BOTTLES.

Cloche
Usually made from glass or plastic, these can be tunnel-shaped to fit over rows of plants, or individual to place over single specimens and protect them from frost and cold.

Compost
For seeds and cuttings (see page 30).

Dibber
Used to create individual holes for seed sowing or inserting cuttings.

Fork and spade
Necessary for digging up plants when it comes to dividing rootballs, bulbs, collecting suckers or material to take root cuttings from.

Fridge
Some seeds require a period of cold dormancy to germinate in spring. This process, called stratification, means seeds may need to be placed in a fridge to recreate the cold of winter.

Garden knife
For cutting softwood and for leaf and root cuttings. If you want to do budding or grafting there are specific types to purchase.

A FREE CLOCHE ALTERNATIVE IS TO CUT THE TOPS OFF PLASTIC BOTTLES AND USE THE REMAINDER TO COVER SMALL PLANTS.

CHOOSE A PEAT-FREE COMPOST.

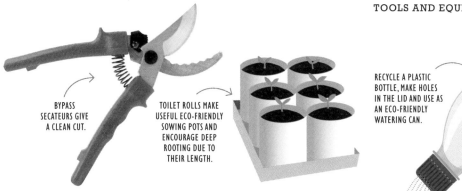

BYPASS SECATEURS GIVE A CLEAN CUT.

TOILET ROLLS MAKE USEFUL ECO-FRIENDLY SOWING POTS AND ENCOURAGE DEEP ROOTING DUE TO THEIR LENGTH.

RECYCLE A PLASTIC BOTTLE, MAKE HOLES IN THE LID AND USE AS AN ECO-FRIENDLY WATERING CAN.

Labels and pens
So you can remember what seeds or cuttings you have! Use indelible ink that won't get washed off by the rain, or a pencil, because you can then rub off the writing and reuse the labels next year.

Lights for propagators
Natural light such as by a window or in a greenhouse is best, but if light is limited, such as in winter, or you are growing in an apartment with few windows, then horticultural lights can be set up to provide it artificially. You may find secondhand ones.

Paper bags and envelopes
Bags are useful for collecting seeds in from the garden; envelopes are perfect for storing seeds in once they have been harvested.

Pots, modules and seed trays
Necessary for planting your seeds into – see how to make your own pots on page 26. If you have lots of seed trays it might be worth building or investing in shelving or seed tray racks so that you can grow plenty of plants without taking up too much room.

Propagators
A propagator is a small warm box used to grow seedlings in to encourage germination. Some propagators are insulated boxes with clear lids to act as a tiny greenhouse (see page 28 for how to make your own). Others can be plugged in, provide bottom heat or might have a thermostat. Choose or make a propagator with enough space to accommodate the height of your plants.

Secateurs
Useful for taking cuttings. Bypass secateurs usually give a better, cleaner cut than anvil types, which tend to crush the stem.

String line
If sowing directly into seed drills or inserting cuttings outside, a string can be pulled taut between two posts to ensure the line is straight.

Watering can
Essential for watering seedlings or cuttings. Ideally a rose should be attached to the nozzle as this produces a fine spray that shouldn't damage seedlings.

MAKE YOUR OWN BIODEGRADABLE POTS

It's essential to have lots of pots for propagating free plants. However, there is no need to rush out to the shops and buy some, as simple pots are easy to make from repurposed newspaper.

IT IS POSSIBLE TO BUY A GADGET (A POT MAKER) THAT HELPS YOU MOULD THE NEWSPAPER INTO POTS, BUT IT IS JUST AS EASY TO MAKE THEM USING AN OLD JAR OR GLASS.

Getting ready

Gather some old newspapers and choose a container to act as your 'mould'. A jam jar is ideal, but as long as it's a rigid container, anything of a similar size will do.

You will need:
- Jam jar or glass
- Newspaper
- Compost
- Plant or seed
- Watering can

1 Take a sheet of newspaper and fold it in half. Fold the sheet in half again in the same direction so you are left with a long strip of folded newspaper 15–20cm (6–8in) wide.

2 Lay your roll of newspaper on a table and place your jar or glass on top at one end, with about 2.5cm (1in) available, overlapping the open end of the jar.

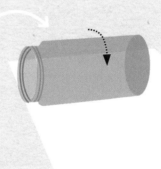

3 Roll the newspaper around the jar then tuck the 2.5cm (1in) overlapping excess newspaper into the open end.

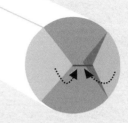

4 Gently pull out the can or jar with one hand, holding the paper roll with the other. Fold down the top 2cm (¾in) of paper into the pot, to hold the pot's shape. For newspaper, this is all it takes to keep the pot in shape. If you are using more rigid card, it is more likely to spring apart, so tie some twine around the middle to keep it in place (this is easier before you remove the jar).

5 Fill the pot with compost and sow your seed or add your cutting. When it comes to planting seedlings out in the garden, there is no need to remove them from the pot. Plant both seedling and pot together. The newspaper will rot in the ground.

MAKE A PROPAGATOR

Propagators are useful for creating extra warmth and providing protection for your seedlings and cuttings. Whilst some seeds will germinate naturally without too much heat, others require a bit more mollycoddling and need to be kept nice and snug.

Getting ready

Fruit punnets from supermarkets are ideal to use as mini-propagators, creating a perfectly warm, moist place for your free plants to grow. If you wish to monitor the temperature, a basic thermometer can be placed inside the box.

You will need:
- Recycled plastic fruit punnet
- Recycled toilet-roll tubes or egg cartons
- Masking or packing tape
- Seed compost

Increase the heat: Some seeds require even more bottom heat than just the cosy warmth of a snug propagator. In this case, if your heating is on, place the propagator on shelves just above warm, but not hot, radiators. The tops of radiator covers are ideal.

1 Join two fruit punnets by taping them long-edge together, forming a 'hinge' that can be opened and closed. One of these will be the base and the other the lid to keep the plants nice and warm.

PROPAGATORS CAN BE PURCHASED BUT A BASIC ONE IS EASY TO CONSTRUCT FROM RECYCLED MATERIALS AND COSTS VERY LITTLE.

2a The easiest method of using the propagator is to fill one of the punnets with seed compost, sow seeds onto the surface, cover lightly with more compost, water, then close the lid. Place the propagator on a sunny windowsill and open the lid if it gets too hot inside.

2b Another method is to pack the propagator full of toilet-roll tubes. The advantage of using these is that the rolls can be planted directly into the garden when they are ready, without having to disturb the roots. The carboard rots once in the soil. Alternatively, use cardboard egg cartons for sowing into, although you may need to cut the cartons to fit in the propagator.

3 Seedlings may need to be watered each day, particularly if placed on a warm windowsill or above a radiator. The easiest way to do this is to place the propagators on a tray to catch any drips. Close its 'lid' afterwards if temperatures are about to dip.

CHOOSING THE RIGHT COMPOST

The type of compost or soil in which a plant grows can be key to its survival. There are a number of different types available, but it is all fairly straightforward once you get started. Composts generally fall into two categories: ones that contain soil (loam) and ones that do not.

CHECK THE 'BEST BEFORE' OR MANUFACTURE DATES. THE FRESHER THE BETTER. OLDER COMPOSTS COULD HAVE LEACHED OR LOST VALUABLE NUTRIENTS OVER TIME.

SOIL-BASED COMPOSTS

Composts that contain soil (loam) are often used for seed sowing and cuttings. They are also used for plants that are going to be planted in a container for more than one year. There are generally three categories of soil or loam-based composts, each one suitable for different stages of your plant's life cycle:

• **Seed compost** – these contain the least amount of nutrients and are suitable for getting seeds and cuttings started. This mix is occasionally referred to as John Innes No 1, although alternatives are available.

• **Potting compost** – this is ideal for potting on your seedlings and cuttings for their next stage of growing (similar mixes are sometimes called John Innes No 2).

• **Container compost** – this is the final stage for plants if using soil or loam-based compost and contains the most amount of nutrients (sometimes referred to as a John Innes No 3 mix).

SEED COMPOST

POTTING COMPOST

CONTAINER COMPOST

COIR COMPOST

PEAT-FREE COMPOST

Always buy peat-free compost to protect the ever-diminishing peatlands. There are lots of alternative peat-free composts available, including coir, bracken and wooden or wool fibres.

OTHER INGREDIENTS

Various materials can be added to improve drainage and water-retaining qualities. The ratio will vary, but four parts compost to one part other ingredient is a good guide.

• **Leaf mould** – to retain moisture. To make, decompose fallen autumn leaves in a bag or container for 6–12 months.

• **Horticultural grit** – to improve drainage; use four parts compost to one part grit.

• **Vermiculite** – to retain moisture. Seeds can be sown directly into it, or try a 50:50 mix with a seed compost.

• **Perlite** – to improve drainage and aerate compost. Use four parts compost to one part vermiculite for most plants, but at 50:50 for cactus and succulents.

Vermiculite and perlite are the least sustainable choices.

VERMICULITE

PERLITE

HORTICULTURAL GRIT

WHERE TO GROW YOUR PLANTS

To grow free plants, you don't necessarily need a garden. All you need is a small surface indoors or outside to put your plants onto, enough light, and protection from creatures such as slugs and snails. Then let nature work its magic, transforming your seeds and cuttings into beautiful plants.

GREENHOUSE

With transparent sides and a roof, glasshouses are perfectly designed to allow the maximum amount of light to reach plants. The range of plants you can grow will depend on whether you decide to heat it or not. This is important in winter if growing houseplants and tender plants.

Most heaters are electric, and some have thermostats and timers (or you can plug these in separately). If you do not have a heater, consider recycling bubble wrap and placing it either around the pots or around the glasshouse. Sheets of fleece can also be used to provide extra protection.

During summer you could hang shade netting on the inside of the roof and the side of the greenhouse that receives the most amount of sun to prevent seedlings from getting scorched through the glass. Alternatively, a 'shade' paint can be applied to the panes of glass, to be washed off in autumn.

COLD FRAME

If you do not have room for a greenhouse, consider a cold frame. These are usually low-level structures with brick or wooden sides and a glass top. Seedlings and cuttings can be placed inside, providing protection. They are often used for hardening off seedlings in spring before planting them outside but can also be used to propagate plants to get them off to an early start.

WINDOWSILL

One of the best places to grow seedlings and cuttings is a windowsill. They are usually warm and receive lots of light, although you may need to be careful that leaves do not get scorched if in direct sunlight such as on a south-facing window.

KITCHEN TABLE

There is nothing wrong with using the kitchen table, or for that matter any indoor table. They are at a comfortable height for working, protected from the cold elements and should receive enough ambient light.

5 THINGS PLANTS NEED

Plants can be grown almost anywhere, so long as you ensure the following five requirements are met. If you provide these, it should be easy to grow plants for free from either seeds or cuttings.

1 Light

2 Air

3 Water

4 Nutritious growing medium

5 Growing space

STARTING YOUR FREE-PLANT JOURNEY

Getting the gardening bug is a wonderful thing as you learn to grow plants and meet like-minded people along the way. Along this journey your garden will slowly fill up with beautiful plants to grace your beds and borders. And the great news is that adding to your burgeoning plant collection can be inexpensive or even free. So, where to start?

CLOSE TO HOME

The best place to start is your own garden. If there are plants you like, you could bulk up existing ones to fill up spaces in flowerbeds, or propagate to swap with other people. If you are not sure which plants you have, then ask friends to identify them, or look them up in books. Chances are they will be common ones and easy to identify. There are also phone apps that help identity plants if you take a photo. If you are still not sure, post photos online on gardening social media sites.

RESEARCH AND RETURN

Once you know what the plant is, you can research the best way to propagate it. In most cases the time when you see a plant that you like and the correct time to propagate from it will be different. Usually when a plant looks its best its seed will not be ready, or the plant will be in full growth and so cannot be dug up and divided. Some cuttings will be okay to take, but you will probably need a return visit. Take photos of plants and make a list so you remember what they are and why you liked them.

FRIENDS AND FAMILY

The next best place to get hold of free plants is your friends and family. Visit their gardens and make a list of the plants you like. If possible, visit a few times in the year, as some plants will be at their best in different seasons to others. Most people will allow you to take seeds and cuttings. After all it does not cost them anything, and you can always offer to propagate a few plants for them too.

FURTHER AFIELD

It is not just your friends' and family's gardens that can be a useful source of free plants. There are plenty of options to find like-minded people keen to collect and swap seeds with you. If you want to take cuttings from other people's gardens – public or private – then always ask first.

PLANT FAIRS AND SEED SWAPS

These can be an excellent place to swap seeds and cuttings, as well as exchange growing tips and advice from other gardeners. It's also an opportunity to get rid of seeds that you may have too many of and get hold of exciting new varieties.

FORUMS AND ONLINE RESOURCES

These can be a good way of extending your network for acquiring plant material, and there are often lots of other site members who are generous with their gardening tips. Their information can be invaluable as you go about acquiring plants for free.

BE EQUIPPED

Remember to take tools with you when you visit to collect plant material for propagating. Some plants will be best to propagate by dividing, so you will need a spade or fork to dig them up. You will also need something to put the plant in to stop the roots drying out, and to ensure it does not make a mess in the back of your car. Spare pots, a bag or a sheet of hessian to wrap the roots in are ideal. Some plants will be propagated by seeds or cuttings, so you will need secateurs and bags to collect the plant material in. Don't forget to take labels and a pen to record what you have collected.

Plant fairs are an opportunity to acquire new plants and seeds, giving you more material for propagating next year.

MAKING A SMALL PROFIT

You may well find that you are so successful with propagating free plants that you have a few surplus plants or seeds on your hands. If this is the case, you could find yourself profiting from your hobby. You will be amazed how many people will buy plants to take home if they look pretty and are for sale at a good price.

If you have security concerns about an honesty box you could ask people to post money through your letterbox instead.

ON DISPLAY

- Plants are easiest to sell when they look good and are in full flower.

- Take care that your plants are looking their best. Remove any browning foliage and fading flowers.

- Try to make the surrounding display look good. Use attractive posters, signs and labels, and perhaps a nice tablecloth laid across your table.

- Display taller plants at the back and smaller plants at the front.

- Make it as easy as possible for people passing by to purchase plants. If possible, have free recycled bags on the table for them to be able to take purchases away.

HONESTY BOX

If you have surplus plants you can set up a stall outside your house with an honesty box. This works well if you are on a popular road with regular passersby. Everyone likes a bargain. Remember to collect your honesty box at the end of each day.

BOOT SALES AND PLANT FAIRS

For car boot sales and plant fairs, you will have to pay a small fee for the stall, though you should easily recoup the initial cost and return a small profit.

PRICING

These plants have cost you nothing, except perhaps for some time and compost, so price them to sell. Also, remember people are unlikely to have much loose change. Price at rounded-off amounts, and avoid traditional retail pricing such as £3.95.

SELLING ONLINE

It is also possible to sell plants online on various commercial websites. Alternatively, you can try setting up your own website, which would save you some commission fees, although the hosting site might still take a cut for every sale. Be aware there are legislation and rules regarding posting and moving plants around domestically and abroad. Check your government's website for any required documentation and relevant legislation.

PLANT BREEDERS' RIGHTS

It is worth being aware of Plant Breeders' Rights (PBR) if considering propagating plants and selling them. Some plants are protected by law, meaning that only the breeder and people granted permission are allowed to reproduce the plant and sell it commercially. It is usually done by the nursery and plant breeders who have bred an exciting new variety, and PBR is there to protect their intellectual rights. The rights usually last for 20 years, or 25 years for trees and vines. If you look carefully on a plant label in a garden centre you will see PBR in brackets if it is registered.

You might breed a special or unusual plant yourself when collecting seed that does not come true. In which case, you might want to apply for PBR if you wish to sell it, to ensure nobody else can exploit it commercially. You would need to register a unique name for the plant and apply via the government website.

Donations welcome: You could always ask for a donation instead of setting a price – you might be pleasantly surprised!

CHAPTER 2

DIVIDE AND CONQUER

Dividing plants is one of the easiest methods of getting plants for free. In addition, it hardly requires any tools. In many cases you just need a spade to dig the plant up. Another advantage to dividing plants is that the effect is almost instant. Within just a few minutes of lifting a plant to divide you can end up with numerous extra plants for free.

In this chapter you will find information on the different techniques that can be used to divide plants, depending on the size of the rootball. You will also find information on how to propagate plants from stolons, suckers and runners. Plant profiles detail which ones are suitable for dividing and why they are worth growing. Follow these simple propagation tips, and your garden will quickly start to fill with your favourite plants, all at no cost.

DIVIDING PLANTS

As well as being easy, it is extremely satisfying to split a plant into sections as you are rewarded instantly with lots of free plants to add to your own garden or give away to friends. Even better is the knowledge that your plants will benefit from being divided every few years as it reinvigorates them.

NEW LIFE TO OLD PLANTS

After a few years, a plant can become congested in the centre. This could cause it to produce less flowers or even send up fewer fresh shoots in that area. This can make flower borders look tired and neglected. Dividing the old plant into sections, discarding a tired-looking centre and replanting the healthy fresh sections helps revitalise the flowerbeds.

WHEN TO DIVIDE

The most common time for dividing plants is in early spring, just before the temperature warms up and the plants come into growth. Another popular time is autumn when the top growth is dying back. Keep plants well watered after dividing.

HOW TO DIVIDE

The simplest method of dividing a plant is to carefully dig it up then use a sharp spade to slice down into the rootball and create individual sections. For larger rootballs, leave the plant in the ground and work your way around it, slicing off sections as you go then lifting them out individually.

Depending on the rootball's size, aim for between three to six sections per plant, each between 10 and 20cm (4 and 8in) across. Retain a healthy section of root, and healthy shoots above the plant if the plant is currently in growth. The centre can be dug out and discarded. Plant new sections back into the soil, water and ideally add some fresh compost into the hole. This will help them retain moisture.

OTHER WAYS TO DIVIDE PLANTS

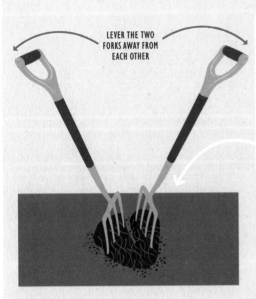

LEVER THE TWO
FORKS AWAY FROM
EACH OTHER

Fork to fork

Dig up the rootball, lay it on the ground and insert two garden forks back to back to each other. Carefully lever the two handles away from each other, which should prise it apart.

Smaller sections

For smaller plants, use a garden knife to cut the rootball up into sections. Some rootballs can even be gently pulled apart to create new plants.

CREATING
NEW PLANTS

Natural look: For a natural planting scheme, use an odd amount of plants – groupings of three or five rather than even numbers – when placing newly divided sections in an herbaceous border.

DIVIDING PERENNIALS

Perennial plants are the mainstay of most people's flower borders. Being perennial means they reappear year after year to reward you with wonderful flowers and foliage. To ensure their display continues to look good, they benefit from being divided every few years.

Daylily *Hemerocallis*

A popular herbaceous perennial for the border, *Hemerocallis* are easy to propagate from by dividing their root system. They are also known as daylilies because each bloom flowers for just one day. Thankfully they produce a rapid succession of lily-like flowers with numerous amounts on each stem, meaning there is a constant and impressive display of fiery rich colours from late spring through to late summer, depending on the variety.

Growing

Plant in fertile soil in full sun, although they will tolerate a moderate amount of shade. They require moist but well-drained soil, so it is worth adding some compost and mulching the surface when planting. If planting more than one, allow about 50cm (20in) between each plant.

Care and maintenance

Fully hardy, they do not require any winter protection. Most daylilies are deciduous and will die back down underground in winter and remerge in the following spring. Once entire individual stems have finished flowering they can be cut back near the base to encourage more stems to grow. Keep an eye out for slugs, which love the emerging shoots.

Propagation

Divide established clumps by digging up the clump in early spring and inserting two forks into the crown 'back to back' (see page 41), carefully prising apart their large fibrous roots. Once in two parts, other sections can be further divided. Slot the new sections back into the flowerbed and keep well watered.

Perennial delphinium

Delphiniums are the quintessential, back-of-the-border, cottage-garden perennial, with their tall flower spikes that add a stately presence to any display in early summer. They come in an attractive range of pastel colours including blue, purple, mauve and white but occasionally there are brighter shades of pink and red.

Growing

Delphiniums thrive in sunny, fertile soil. Make sure each plant is given plenty of space. Check the label as some delphiniums grow to only 45cm (18in) wide, whereas varieties from the Elatum Group can grow to up to 75cm (30in) wide.

Care and maintenance

Perennial delphiniums will need staking in exposed areas to avoid their tall spike blowing over. Once an individual flower spike has finished flowering remove the stem to encourage replacements. In autumn cut back the foliage and mulch the area around the roots.

Propagation

It is easy to propagate perennial delphiniums by division. When plants are three or more years old, dig them up and slice the rootball into three or four new plants with a sharp spade. Discard the old centre and replant the new sections.

THREE TO TRY

Delphinium **Black Knight Group** – grows up to 1.8m (6ft) tall and produces striking spikes of semi-double, blue-purple flowers with black centres in summer.

Delphinium **Summer Skies Group** – tall flower spikes up to 1.8m (6ft) high with powder-blue flowers and white centres.

Delphinium **'Faust'** – long spikes of deep blue-purple, semi-double flowers with dark centres, grows up to 1.8m (6ft) high.

Black-eyed Susan *Rudbeckia*

Rudbeckias are a late-summer flowering perennial with daisy-like flowers with a dark centre and petals that are predominantly yellow but can include oranges, bronzes and reds.

Growing
Plant flowers in spring in fertile, well-drained soil in full sun. They will tolerate some shade but will produce fewer flowers. Heights can vary between about 30cm and 2m (12in and 6½ft) so check for planting distances.

Propagation
Rudbeckias are best divided by digging up in early spring, using a spade, before replanting the new sections.

Bergamot *Monarda didyma*

Grown by many for its scented foliage, which is used to make Oswego tea. It is an herbaceous perennial with pink, white or red flowers surrounded by impressive bracts. The bees love these flowers, hence the other common name, bee balm.

Growing
Plant in full sun or dappled shade. Bergamots can be prone to mildew though if the roots dry out, so keep well watered. Although a perennial, bergamots are often grown by gardeners for just one or two years before discarding or propagating.

Propagation
They can be propagated by dividing their roots in spring, using a spade to divide clumps, as well as by collecting and sowing their seed.

Christmas rose *Hellebore*

A popular, low-growing perennial with nodding flower heads that appear in late winter, often lasting until mid-spring. Also known as Lenten roses, although flowering is usually sometime between the festive season and Easter.

Growing

Growing up to about 40cm (16in) high, they are happiest growing in light shade, although the species *H. foetidus* (stinking hellebore) prefers deeper shade. Unusually for a herbaceous perennial, their leathery leaves often do not die back completely underground in winter but instead remain visible throughout the year. Flowers are usually black, white, pink or purple.

Propagation

Hellebores are best divided in autumn. Dig the plants up and prise them apart with a gardening knife. Less-established clumps may pull apart by hand; well-established clumps may require an axe!

New Zealand flax *Phormium tenax*

Foliage plants with long, strap-shaped leaves in a range of bright and sometimes stripy forms. They are tough plants that can go without watering for long periods – some of the smaller dwarf types are grown in containers for this reason.

Growing

They prefer well-drained soil in full sun and are relatively low maintenance once in the ground and established. Just occasionally remove dead leaves and the flower spike once it has finished flowering.

Propagation

The best way to propagate them is to split the rootball using a sharp spade. Some of the more established plants may have a large rootball, so it can be less back-breaking to just slice off sections around the edge with a spade rather than trying to lift the entire rootball out for splitting.

FLAX ARE POPULAR ADDITIONS FOR GARDEN BORDERS AS PART OF SUB-TROPICAL PLANTING SCHEMES OR AMONGST ORNAMENTAL GRASSES.

DIVIDING TUBERS

Not all plants grew from a system of woody or fibrous roots. Some grow from underground swollen tubers, bulbs, corms and rhizomes instead, which store their nutrients.

Dahlia

Dahlias are one of the stars of the late summer border. The flower heads come in a range of elaborate shapes and colours including types known as cactus, pompon, anemone and waterlily.

Growing

Originating from Mexico, dahlias love to bask in the sun and should be planted in fertile soil that is moist yet well drained. Dahlias are perennials, producing tubers, which are used to store food for the plant. After one or two years the tubers can become congested and benefit from being thinned out.

Propagation

As dahlias are slightly tender, in colder regions they are lifted in autumn and stored over winter, before being planted outside again in spring. This is an ideal opportunity to divide out the tubers, which can be done any time between late autumn and early spring. It is easier to see the tuber 'eyes' in early spring as they start to swell when the weather warms up. Each tuber must contain an eye to grow.

POMPON DAHLIA

DIVIDING CLUMPS OF DAHLIA TUBERS

1 Inspect the clump of dahlias and look for swollen eyes, which will be near the section of tuber where they are attached. Give them a squeeze to ensure they are solid and not soft and rotting.

2 Use a sharp knife and cut the individual tuber, severing it from the main clump by the crown, ensuring that the eye near that end is included and not damaged. If the tuber does not have an eye it will not grow.

3 Place the individual tubers into shallow trays of peat-free potting compost and cover over with more compost so that they are just below the surface.

4 As the weather starts to warm up, inspect the tubers and look for shoots emerging from the eyes. When the shoots are about 5cm (2in) long they are ready to be lifted from the compost and planted outside.

5 When the risk of frost is over, the tubers can be planted in the ground. Lie them flat, ensuring that the new shoots are pointing upwards. Tubers do not need to be planted deeply, just a couple of centimetres below the surface.

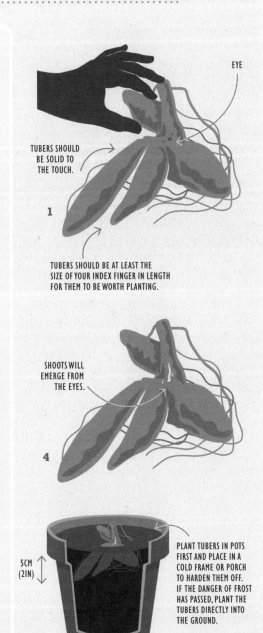

EYE

TUBERS SHOULD BE SOLID TO THE TOUCH.

1

TUBERS SHOULD BE AT LEAST THE SIZE OF YOUR INDEX FINGER IN LENGTH FOR THEM TO BE WORTH PLANTING.

SHOOTS WILL EMERGE FROM THE EYES.

4

5CM (2IN)

PLANT TUBERS IN POTS FIRST AND PLACE IN A COLD FRAME OR PORCH TO HARDEN THEM OFF. IF THE DANGER OF FROST HAS PASSED, PLANT THE TUBERS DIRECTLY INTO THE GROUND.

DIVIDING BULBS

Plants that grow from bulbs can often be lifted and divided, which is an easy way to increase the flower display the following year. This can be done when they are dormant or when they are in growth. Bulbs can also be divided by scaling and chipping, as described on pages 50–51.

Snowdrops *Galanthus nivalis*

The appearance of the demure, bell-shaped, nodding heads of white snowdrop flowers heralds the arrival of early spring, although there are a few varieties that will flower in autumn. This perennial is fully hardy and can even push through frosty or frozen ground.

Propagation

The best time to propagate snowdrops is in spring just after they have finished flowering and are still in leaf. The technique involves dividing the bulbs while they are actively growing and is called lifting in the green.

Ideal position: If you are looking for a new area for your snowdrops, remember they prefer dappled shade in moist but well-drained soil.

OTHER BULBS TO DIVIDE

- Daffodils
- Crocus (although technically a corm it is the same procedure)
- Winter aconites
- Wood anemones
- Hyacinth

DIVIDING SNOWDROP BULBS

1 Use a garden spade to dig around existing clumps of snowdrops, taking care not to damage the bulbs or separate them from their leaves.

2 Once clumps have been dug up they can be divided by hand. Either make smaller clumps out of them or separate them out as individual bulbs.

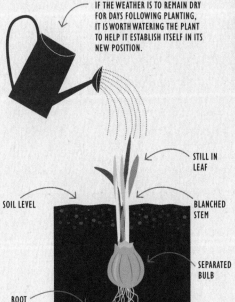

IF THE WEATHER IS TO REMAIN DRY FOR DAYS FOLLOWING PLANTING, IT IS WORTH WATERING THE PLANT TO HELP IT ESTABLISH ITSELF IN ITS NEW POSITION.

STILL IN LEAF

SOIL LEVEL

BLANCHED STEM

SEPARATED BULB

ROOT

3 Plant the bulbs in new planting holes. To put them in at the correct depth, look for where the stem was blanched (white) from its former planting position and bury them in soil to the same level.

4 Try to make either clumps or individual bulbs look as natural as possible, avoiding symmetrical blocks or straight rows.

SCALING AND CHIPPING

Almost any bulb can be propagated by scaling or chipping. Scaling is a process suitable for scaly bulbs like lilies or fritillaries. Chipping is for bulbs that are not scaly. It is easy to do, requiring very few tools and just a bit of patience – it can take a few months before the new baby bulbs (bulblets) are ready to plant out.

BULBLET

SCALING

Scaling is suitable for most types of lily bulbs and it's a useful way to extend the amount of these beautiful flowers if you already have them growing in the garden.

You will need:
- Bulbs
- Sharp knife and chopping board
- Seed tray
- Seed or potting compost
- 7.5cm (3in) pots and seed trays

1 Wait for the bulbs to die back and go dormant before lifting. Work your way around the bulb, peeling off the scales, ensuring each one has a section of the basal plate with it.

2 Leave them to dry overnight then place in a bag filled with moist potting compost, leaving them in a warm, dark place indoors. Check regularly to ensure they are not going mouldy.

3 After a few weeks the little bulblets start to grow near the base of the bulb. Place them in larger pots filled with potting compost to give them room to grow. Discard any scales that have not formed bulblets. There is no need to remove the bulblets from the scales at this stage.

4 Cover the scales with bulblets with about 2cm (¾in) of potting compost and move them somewhere cooler.

5 They will start to send up shoots. When they have finished growing and are dying back, they can be pulled up and planted out separately either in individual pots or in the garden and grown on for another year to allow the bulbs to fully develop.

CHIPPING

This is suitable for a variety of different bulbs including: alliums, hyacinths, nerines, hippeastrum, daffodils, irises and fritillaries.

You will need:
- Bulbs
- Sharp knife and chopping board
- Seed tray
- Seed or potting compost
- 7.5cm (3in) pots and seed trays

1 Using your fingers, remove the loose, wrinkly outer skin of the bulb. Ensure the bulbs are healthy, firm and of the standard size you would expect for the type of bulb you are wanting to grow.

2 Take a sharp knife and carefully cut the growing tip off the bulb.

3 Trim off the roots but take care not to damage the basal plate, which is essential for this method of propagation to work.

4 Turn the bulb upside down, placing it on a surface or chopping board so the basal plate faces upwards (as shown in the photograph, right).

5 Cut downwards through the bulb into sections (chips), ensuring that each segment has a part of the basal plate attached. Expect to get between four and eight chops per bulb.

6 Leave the chips to dry out overnight then place in a bag, cover with a mix of 10 parts horticultural grit to 1 part water and leave in a warm dark place at about 20°C (68°F).

7 During the next 12 weeks the scales (layers) within the chips will start to separate and bulblets will start to form just above the basal plate.

8 Remove the chips from the bag and place them individually with the basal plate covered in potting compost and the remainder just above the surface.

9 The exposed section of the chip will rot away and the foliage and shoots of the new plant will start to appear.

10 When they are a few centimetres high they can be planted outside or into the environment where they would usually grow.

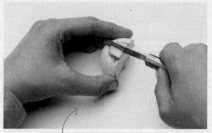

5   THE BASAL PLATE SHOULD BE FACING UPWARDS.

NEW PLANTS FROM RUNNERS, SUCKERS AND STOLONS

Other ingenious ways that plants have found to grow and spread throughout the garden include sending out stolons, runners and suckers. As gardeners, we can harness these natural growing habits and use them to our advantage by propagating from each of these parts.

SUCKERS

Some shrubs and trees, such as lime trees (*Tillia*), sweet box (*Sarcococca*), some rose species, glory flower (*Clerodendrum bungei*) and raspberries, have a tendency to send out suckers from just below the soil, from which it is easy to produce free new plants. They are easy to propagate from if they can be detached carefully from the main plant with some roots.

Propagating from suckers

• Carefully dig around the sucker with a fork to expose the fibrous roots, taking care not to damage the original tree.
• Use secateurs or a sharp knife to sever it from the main plant.
• Trim any straggling or overextended roots so that just a healthy clump of fibrous roots remains.
• Cut back the sucker by about half to reduce the stress on the potential new plant.
• Plant the sucker with its roots at the same depth as it was originally in the ground.

Raspberries are easy to propagate from suckers. In autumn dig them up and plant them in pots of compost, ready to plant outside in spring.

Common lilac *Syringa vulgaris*

Lilacs are deciduous shrubs producing shades of violet, purple, pink or white flowers in late spring and early summer. They have attractive heart-shaped leaves.

Growing
Lilacs prefer neutral to slightly alkaline soil conditions and are ideal shrubs if your garden is on chalk soil.

Care and maintenance
Fairly easy to maintain, lilacs do freely produce suckers in the surrounding soil throughout the growing season, which may need removing if they are encroaching on other nearby plants.

Propagation
It is easy to propagate from softwood cuttings in summer, but an even more effective method is to use the suckers from around its base to produce new plants. Excavate the soil around the sucker and carefully dig it up, ensuring it is attached to as much of the root system as possible. Either place it in a new pot with lots of peat-free potting compost or find an area of the garden to plant it into.

Propagating from suckers: Make sure that it is not a grafted plant. Check the original plant label, or look for a swollen joint on the stem, usually just above ground level where the plant was joined to a root system. Otherwise you will just be propagating the rootstock and not your desired plant. The rootstock is a different plant to the above-ground plant that it is grafted onto. A few rootstocks tend to send out suckers.

STOLONS

Stolons are shoots that tend to arch or run along the ground producing a new plant at the end, such as a gooseberry. However, some stolons run just under the surface of the soil (such as mint) and root at their nodes.

To propagate from a stolon

• Cut stolons into 10–15cm (4–6in) lengths. Ensure there are a few nodes on each section (dormant or growing buds).
• Place them in seed compost in individual pots or seed trays at 1cm (½in) apart.
• Stolons should be buried close to the surface and do not like being too deep.
• When the individual stolons are actively growing they can be moved into bigger pots or planted in the garden.

RUNNERS

Runners are similar to stolons but their exploratory roots tend to be more slender. They grow overground and produce roots at their nodes and eventually small plants. Plants that spread by runners include strawberries, some potentillas and bugle (*Ajuga reptans*).

To propagate a runner

• Fill a pot with peat-free general purpose compost and place it near the plant to be propagated.
• Use a peg to pin down a runner into the pot, ensuring the new roots are in contact with the compost.
• Once the runner is producing fresh new leaves, use secateurs to cut the runner close to the new plant.
• The new plant can then be planted out in the garden.

Strawberry plants produce lots of runners that can be removed and planted in compost to grow into new plants.

STRAWBERRY RUNNER

Strawberry
Fragaria x *ananassa*

Strawberries are the quintessential summer fruit, producing delicious, juicy red berries that can be enjoyed with cream or made into most people's favourite jam.

Growing

Apart from the fruit, another reason for growing strawberry plants is that they take up hardly any space in the garden, making them suitable for containers and planters. Thanks to their trailing habit they also look great in hanging baskets. Strawberries need to be grown in full sun in sheltered, fertile but well-drained soil. Keep young plants watered once removed from the main plant.

Propagation

Propagation of the runners is easy (see opposite), meaning that new, healthy strawberries can be produced each year. Strawberries are perennial but are more fruitful if replaced with newly propagated plants every two or three years. Alpine or wild strawberries tend not to produce runners and should therefore be propagated by seed instead.

Common mint
Mentha officinalis

Grown primarily for the aromatic, fresh-flavoured foliage, mint produces an attractive blue flower from mid- to late summer. There is a massive array of different-flavoured mints including ginger mint, chocolate mint and lavender mint, as well as traditional spearmints, peppermints and apple mints.

Growing

Mint is one of the easiest plants to grow in the garden. In fact, it is almost too easy and if you aren't careful, it can spread throughout beds using its underground stems, or stolons, to do this. Due to this exuberant growth habit, it is recommended to grow mint in a container or raised bed.

Propagation

Mint can simply be divided by pulling clumps apart, but the other technique is to take lots of 10cm (4in) sections of the stolon and plant them horizontally in seed trays or pots, covering them with potting compost so that they are just below the surface. Once shoots have started to appear they can be planted into their final position.

MINT WILL TAKE OVER YOUR FLOWERBED. IT IS ADVISABLE TO GROW IT IN POTS, CONTAINERS OR RAISED BEDS INSTEAD SO THAT IT IS CONTAINED.

CHAPTER 3

GROWING FROM SEED

Growing your own plants from tiny seeds can feel like a magical experience. Plants of all shapes and sizes can be grown in this way. It's incredible to think that even a mighty oak tree began its life as a tiny acorn. Although nature does most of the hard work, we can still give seeds a helping hand to grow into new and healthy plants by harvesting them, providing them with the right conditions and nurturing them to full size. With a bit of know-how you can fill your garden for free by collecting seed from either your own outdoor space or from friends and family.

This chapter gives you all the information you need to grow your own plants from seed. From how to harvest seed and store it correctly, to different techniques for sowing seeds and how to care for them once they have germinated. There are also numerous profiles of plants suitable for growing from seed, so that you can select ones that will look good in your garden.

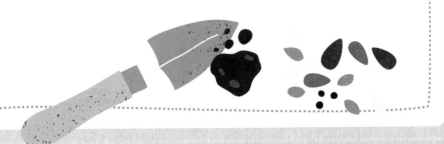

COLLECTING SEEDS

Gathering seeds from your favourite plants is a wonderful way of preserving your garden flowers so they continue to grow for you year after year. Not only is it rewarding but it will save you money as you will not need to buy replacement plants annually. Alternatively, if you have friends and family with plants that you like, you can add to your garden collection by harvesting their seeds.

WHEN TO HARVEST

Seeds should have been given enough time to ripen on the plant before being picked. The average time for seed to be ready is about two months after flowering. All plants vary, but most are ready when the flowers start to fade and the seeds turn from green to brown, although ripe seeds can be other colours too such as red or black.

Some seeds ripen inside fruits such as berries and drupes, in which case the seed is usually ripe when the fruit is ready for eating or starting to drop from the tree.

Other seeds ripen in pods or cases that can often split and change colour when the seed is ready.

HYBRID AND F1 SEEDS

Did you know F1 is an abbreviation for Filial 1, meaning 'first children'? If collecting seed from F1 or hybrid plants, the new seedlings will not come true and will have variations from the parents. F1 seeds are specially bred by plant breeders to create a variety from two parent plants with desired traits such as higher yields, better vigour and plant resistance. F1 hybrids are usually more expensive than other seeds as the process of producing them is quite laborious.

Birds like seeds too! It's wise to cover your favourite plants with a net until you are ready to collect the seeds.

Dry is best: Try to harvest seeds on a dry day. If they are wet they may well rot once they are in storage.

SEED TYPES

Seeds come in many different guises.

DRUPE

PEA PODS

CAPSULE

BERRY

FOLLICLE

CONE

WINGED SEEDS

HOW TO SOW SEEDS

There are numerous different methods of sowing seeds. Some are sown directly into the soil, whilst others are better sown in pots or seed trays. The size of the seed can also make a difference as to how they are treated. Here you will find some of the main techniques used when growing plants from seed.

DIRECT SOWING

Seedlings that do not like to have their roots disturbed as they establish are best sown directly where they are to grow, either in pots or in the open ground.

SCATTER SEED OVER LARGE AREAS TO CREATE A WILDFLOWER BED OR GARDEN. BUY AS A MIX OR MIX YOUR OWN.

Seed mix: If the seed is very small, mix with sand for an even distribution.

ON A SMALLER SCALE, SMALL SEEDS CAN ALSO BE BROADCAST IN CONTAINERS ON THE PATIO (DIRECT).

SEEDLINGS CAN BE THINNED OUT AND THE REMAINING ONES LEFT TO GROW AND DEVELOP TO THEIR FULL SIZE.

HOW TO SOW OUTSIDE

Broadcasting seed

This direct sowing technique is often used when sowing grass or wildflower mixes. The seeds are scattered, or broadcast, over the surface soil, then lightly raked in. For larger areas, it is a good idea to mark out a system of 1 x 1m (3 x 3ft) grids with string to get a consistent spread of seeds. To ensure an even spread, sow half the recommended rate according to information on packets or in books and on websites, in one direction, then the other half at a 90-degree angle to it.

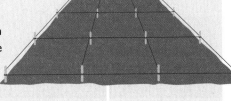

Drill trenches or rows

Seeds sown directly into drills made in the soil or compost is a method used for veg growing, where crops are grown in straight lines for easy tending, and for small seeds such as carrot and parsnip. Make shallow trenches or rows using the edge of a hoe or the tip of a bamboo cane. Stretch string between two bamboo canes or posts for a straight line.

Dibbed holes

Some seeds, usually larger types such as beans, peas, sweetcorn and hardy annual flowers including sweet peas and sunflowers, are sown directly into the soil in individual holes. A dibber is often used to create these holes, although the end of a bamboo cane or even a pencil can be used if you do not own a dibber.

INDIRECT SOWING

Sowing seeds in pots or modules, to be transplanted to their final position later, allows for more tender plants to have a longer growing season as they can be sown indoors whilst the weather is cold outside.

Hardening off

Plants grown under cover will often need 'hardening off' before being planted in the garden. This is because the shock of moving from inside to outside can damage the vulnerable seedlings. Some gardeners use a cold frame (see page 32) for hardening off for a few days, but if you do not have one, then a sheltered place outdoors such as a porch or shed will do. Alternatively, try moving them outside during the day and bring them back in at night for a few days, before finally planting them outside for good.

PRICKING OUT

Pricking out is the term used for removing seedlings when they are tiny and planting them into an individual pot to give them more room to grow and develop. Take care when doing this as the plant is very fragile. Use a dibber or something of a similar size to carefully prise out the seedling. Always hold the plant by a leaf and not the stem when doing this. If the leaf breaks it is not the end of the world, but if the stem breaks you will have probably lost the plant.

Seedlings grown indoors will be tender and need to be hardened off gradually in a porch or cold frame before planting outside permanently.

HOW TO SOW INDOORS

Seed trays and pots

Some smaller seeds are best scattered over the surface of compost in a seed tray. They are then later pricked out into individual pots to give them more room to grow (see box opposite). Larger seeds can be planted individually into modules or pots and placed in a propagator, greenhouse or sunny windowsill and planted out later.

Labelling: Carefully label your plants and include sowing dates.

Root-trainers and gutters

There are also root-trainers that are cleverly designed with long narrow root runs, which unclip to open up all the way down to the root system when they need to be planted out. This avoids disturbing them.

Another technique, suitable when plants are needed to grow in a line, is to sow seeds into lengths of gutter indoors. Once the seeds have germinated and the soil has warmed up outside, the seedlings can be slid out in one section into their final planting place in the soil. This avoids disturbing the roots too much.

REMOVING AND STORING SEEDS

Try to give your seed treasure the best start in life! By gathering and removing seeds with gentle care, being sure to keep them clean, dry and at an appropriate, even temperature, they will be well prepared to grow when the time is right to plant them. This will usually be until the weather warms up (aside from a few seeds such as hellebores, which should be sown immediately).

COLLECTING SEEDS

There are various techniques for collecting seeds. Some larger seedheads might benefit from being cut from the plant with the stalks then held upside down with a paper bag placed over them, then shaken to loosen and catch all the seeds. Others may need removing from a pod and shelled like you would a broad bean or pea. Always remove any debris (the chaff) before storing because these can harbour mould and cause fungus problems for the seeds.

The seeds from berries are best removed from their flesh by crushing them with the back of a spoon into a sieve. Rinse off the flesh and then dry the seeds on kitchen paper.

Exploding seeds (yes, they exist!) such as *Impatiens* and *Oxalis* are best harvested by placing a bag over their seed head and shaken. The seeds will explode into the bag.

STORING SEEDS

Seeds are best collected in paper bags and then stored in envelopes. A sachet of desiccant such as silica gel can be added, which helps absorb the moisture and humidity, reducing the chances of seeds turning mouldy and rotting. A free way to get hold of this gel is from various recycled packaging such as found in shoe boxes.

Once in their envelopes, and labelled, try to keep your seeds stored in a cool environment, avoiding places with temperature fluctuations (such as a conservatory or by a radiator). Many people put them into a drawer or a wooden box.

> **Moist seeds:** Although most seeds should be kept dry, there are a few that will not germinate if they are allowed to dry out. The most common examples are seeds of magnolias, oaks and walnuts, which can be kept in moist compost until ready to sow in their desired position.

STRATIFYING

Some seeds need specific temperatures to break their dormancy. To do this, gardeners use a technique called stratification, which artificially creates a colder or warmer environment for the seeds.

Cold-environment seeds

Seeds that require a cold environment should be placed in a fridge or freezer at a temperature lower than 5°C (41°F), to replicate cold temperatures outside. Place the seeds in a sealed plastic bag containing a mix of compost and vermiculite (see page 31). After a few weeks the seeds will start to sprout and they can then be planted outside.

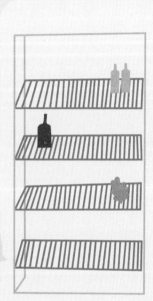

Warm-environment seeds

A similar process can be done for seeds that require a warm environment to germinate, placing them in a warm propagator (see page 28) instead of a fridge.

ANNUAL FLOWER SEEDS

Hardy annuals are easy to grow from seed and provide you with quick results, as they put on a dazzling display in just a few months. There are lots to choose from, including many traditional garden favourites such as sweet peas, love-in-a-mist and sunflowers.

SWEET PEA SEEDS

Sweet pea *Lathyrus odoratus*

Classic cottage-garden plants, these hardy annuals are delightfully fragrant flowers. Most are climbers but there are also shorter trailing types. They can be grown in containers and make great cut-flower displays in the house too.

Sowing

Sow seeds between autumn and spring individually into modules or 9cm (3½in) diameter pots. The earlier the seeds are sown, the earlier they will flower and the longer the flowering season will be. The seeds of a sweet pea are quite thick, so soaking them overnight in water prior to sowing can help soften the outer walls, making germination quicker. Sow in modules or repurposed toilet rolls and plant outside in April. Alternatively, they can be sown directly into the soil from mid to late spring, 3cm (1in) deep with a spacing of 15cm (6in) between each one.

Growing and care

Most sweet peas are climbers growing up to 2m (6½ft) high, and they will therefore need a climbing support for their tendrils to grab hold of and scramble up. The easiest way to do this is to construct a wigwam made of bamboo canes with string spiralled through it. They like fertile growing conditions so add plenty of organic matter into the soil prior to planting. Grow in full sun for their flowers to fully develop their sweetly perfumed aroma. Flowers appear from midsummer through to late summer, although earlier crops are possible if sown in autumn. Pick the flowers regularly to encourage more to bloom.

Picking and harvesting seeds

If collecting seeds for next year, allow the pods to ripen on the plant before harvesting them on a dry day, shelling and storing in envelopes with labels.

Love-in-a-mist *Nigella damascena*

One of the most spectacular looking of all the hardy annuals that can be grown in the garden, the foliage is feathery, and appears to swirl magically around the stem and flower, hence the common name. The plants are easy to grow and often seed naturally, in fact, almost too easily. Once you have sown them in your garden, you may well have them forever with little effort.

Sowing

Love-in-a-mist are quick-growing annuals ideal for filling in gaps in your border. Simply tip the seeds into your hand then scatter them in the soil where you wish them to grow and lightly rake them in. They do require a sunny position in well-drained soil, so it may be necessary to add horticultural grit if your soil is heavy.

Growing and care

Seedlings can be thinned out to a spacing of about 10cm (4in) each once they appear, which will produce bigger, sturdier plants. However, most people let them jostle for position and grow where the seed falls. They will eventually grow to about 50cm (20in) high. Love-in-a-mist are low maintenance and require no staking or other care, except to be kept weed-free.

Picking and harvesting seeds

Seeds from love-in-a-mist are easy to collect and sow again the following spring for another dramatic display the following year. In milder areas, you can even sow in autumn. Love-in-a-mist is so promiscuous, if you already have it in your garden, it will likely spread around freely anyway – a reason why another of its common names is 'sow and forget'.

THREE TO TRY

'Persian Jewels' – attractive mix of flowers including light blue, pink and white.

'Midnight' – dark blue, almost black coloured flowers.

'Delft Blue' – popular variety producing a pretty mix of blue and white flowers.

SEEDS ARE READY TO COLLECT WHEN THE CAPSULE TURNS BROWN.

Sunflower *Helianthus annuus*

SEEDS

Originating from the Americas, sunflowers of any colour and height love a sunny position in the garden. They also require a fertile but well-drained soil.

Sowing

Sunflowers need to be sown each year, ideally in spring in individual 9cm (3½in) pots or sown directly in the ground, after the risk of frost is over. Tall varieties will need staking to prevent them flopping over.

Picking and harvesting seeds

Once they have finished flowering, leave the seeds to ripen (the petals will have dropped and the seeds will look plump and either black or black-and-white). Collect enough to sow and leave the remainder for birds to enjoy. Store seeds in an envelope in a drawer and sow the following spring.

Nasturtium *Tropaeolum majus*

These annual flowering plants produce masses of bright orange, red and yellow flowers. Lesser-known varieties can have salmon pink and cream flowers. They can be trained up wigwams or left to trail over the edges of containers and baskets. They require sun for at least half the day.

Sowing

Sow them in spring in 9cm (3½in) pots and plant them out when they are about 8cm (3in) high, or sow them directly into the soil at 10cm (4in) apart and thin out to 25cm (10in) once they germinate.

Picking and harvesting seeds

Once they have finished flowering, collect the seeds, allow to dry and store somewhere cool and dark such as in a drawer. Sow the following spring.

Common or annual poppy *Papaver rhoeas*

Red annual poppies are associated with Remembrance Day, although there are other species with a wider range of colours, such as Welsh poppy, Iceland poppy and opium poppy. Seeds can lie dormant in the soil for years before germinating, with a reputation for liking disturbed soil.

Sowing

Sow annual poppy seeds in April. Rake over the ground then scatter where you want them to grow. Rake them carefully into the ground. They are quick to grow to their full height of 60cm (24in).

Picking and harvesting seeds

The seeds are set in a capsule that can be shaken into a bag or envelope and either scattered elsewhere on bare ground or stored until April the following year and then sown again.

French marigold *Tagetes patula*

Marigolds are bright and bold with cheery orange and yellow flowers. They grow to 30cm (12in) and are ideal for using in bedding schemes, at the front of a border or in containers and hanging baskets.

Sowing

Seeds are sown in spring in individual 9cm (3½in) pots or modules. Plant them at a 20cm (8in) spacing out in a sunny position in early summer. Alternatively, they can be sown directly in the soil. They will flower from midsummer until the first frosts.

Picking and harvesting seeds

Collect seeds after flowering and store in a cool, dark place. The following spring they can be sown again indoors in pots or directly in the soil once it has warmed up.

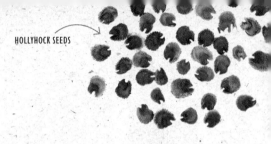

HOLLYHOCK SEEDS

PERENNIAL FLOWER SEEDS

Plants that live for more than two years are classed as perennial. Herbaceous perennials, discussed here, tend to die back in winter. They may take a couple of years to reach flowering age if sown from seed, but once they do, they will reward you with a spectacular display of flowers every year, for years to come.

Hollyhock *Alcea rosea*

Synonymous with cottage gardens, these short-lived perennials flower in the second year after growing from seed. They have tall flower spikes with impressive round leaves. Hollyhocks can grow and seed themselves in the poorest and stoniest of soils.

Sowing
Sow their flat, papery seeds between late winter and mid-spring in seed trays filled with seed compost. Cover the seeds with another thin layer of compost and place in a warm position indoors or in a heated propagator. Seedlings appear between ten days to two weeks later.

Growing and care
When they are about 6cm (2in) tall, carefully prick out into individual pots. Plant outside in May in a sunny position in the garden, in free-draining soil. Due to their height they are best planted at the back of a border.

Propagation
Hollyhocks will produce large trumpet-shaped flowers all up the flower spike. If you leave them on the plant they will produce seeds that can be harvested and stored somewhere dark, dry and cool, and sown again to flower in another two years' time.

African lily *Agapanthus*

Add a touch of the exotic to your borders with these sun-loving South African perennials. Their impressively large, spherical flower heads are usually mid-blue, but can be sky blue, purple, lilac, white and pink, with strap-like leaves that are equally eye-catching.

AGAPANTHUS FLOWER HEAD

Sowing

Plants should be grown in full sun in well-drained soil. Plant individual clumps of agapanthus at a spacing of about 30cm (8in) apart. Many gardeners will remove flower spikes when they go over, to keep the display tidy, but leave a few flower spikes on the plant if you want to propagate from seed. These spent flower spikes can still contribute to the beauty of a flower border.

of black seeds that can be sown straight away. Fill a seed tray with seed compost and sprinkle the seeds lightly over the surface. Add a light dressing of compost. Keep on a warm windowsill over winter and prick out and plant individually into larger pots. Plant them out in the garden or in containers at a spacing of 35cm (14in) apart. They should flower in the second year.

Growing and care

Due to their stout stems and supporting strappy leaves, these low-maintenance plants do not usually require staking. Keep the area weed free and only water in extreme drought, as they are fairly tolerant of most dry conditions.

Propagation

The easiest way of propagating agapanthus is to divide the clumps in spring. However, it can be more fun to collect their seed to propagate from, as they don't come true from seed, and you therefore might get an interesting variation when it grows (see page 58 for more on true seeds). Collect the seed heads when they start to turn brown in late summer. Each capsule contains a number

THREE TO TRY

'Phantom' – violet-blue flowers at the tip fading to white towards the throat.

'Midnight Star' – large, dark flowers reaching 12cm (5in) across.

'Silver Baby' – dwarf variety reaching only 35cm (14in) in height, with white flowers flushed with blue.

Lavender *Lavandula angustifolia*

This popular Mediterranean herb is ideal for edging pathways and for the front of borders. Not only do they look great, but the relatively short-lived shrubs are loved by bees too. As they don't always have a long shelf life, it is good to always have some newly propagated plants in ready supply for when they need replacing.

Sowing

Lavender prefers a light, well-drained soil so add plenty of grit if your soil is heavy or poor draining. Plant at 45cm (18in) spacing if planting in rows, although the size of the plants does vary depending on variety. Plant in full sun to enjoy their aromatic scent.

Growing and care

Lavender is fairly drought tolerant so should not need too much watering during the summer, except for when first planted. Prune twice a year: lightly trim the flower spikes after flowering; then in early spring give the bush a closer trim to shape it, taking care not to cut into the older wood, as it does not regenerate easily from that area.

Propagation

There are various ways lavender can be propagated, including taking cuttings. However, they can also be grown by seed, although the new plants will differ from the original parent plants. Collect seed after flowering and sow into small trays or modules in spring. Plant out the following autumn or spring.

LAVENDER FLOWERS

THREE TO TRY

'**Hidcote**' – compact habit with deep violet-purple flower spikes about 3–4cm (1–1½in) in length.

'**Miss Katherine**' – one of the taller shrubs, reaching up to 75cm (30in), with delicate pink flowers in summer.

Lavandula stoechas **French Lavender, 'Kew Red'** – not as hardy as *angustifolia*, so plant in a sheltered position. This variety has pale pink and dark purple flowers.

Coneflower *Echinacea purpurea*

ECHINACEA SEEDS

A popular herbaceous perennial with a reputation for being a bit short-lived, so it is good to have propagated plants ready to replace retired ones. Also, these plants can be effective in large drifts, so propagating from seed can provide a large number of plants cheaply.

Sowing

Plant in well-drained soil in full sun. Although lack of moisture at the roots can cause these plants to suffer, adding organic matter when planting will help. For maximum impact, plant in large drifts of three or five plants along a border. Alternatively, grow individually in pots. Plant 50cm (20in) apart.

Growing and care

Their upright habit and sturdy stems should mean they do not need staking. After flowering, leave the flowers and seeds for as long as possible to allow the insects to enjoy them. Eventually, they can be tidied up by cutting back to near ground level in spring before their new growth starts.

Propagation

Plants can be divided although they tend to dislike having much root disturbance. They can also have cuttings taken from them in spring. Harvesting seed is easy. Simply collect them in autumn and store safely until spring when they can be sown indoors by sprinkling over compost in seed trays and planted out the following autumn.

THREE TO TRY

'White Swan' – pure white petals and a golden-yellow centre, growing to a maximum height of 60cm (24in).

'Golden Skipper' – compact variety with rich golden flowers, ideal for a garden if short of space.

'Irresistible' – stunning double-flowering variety with impressive pink-orange flowers.

DRIED PEA SEEDS

ANNUAL VEGETABLES AND HERBS

Many of us will like the idea of growing our own food from the garden, but it is even better when you have not even had to buy any seeds. Thankfully, it is easy to collect vegetable and herb seeds at the end of each year and sow them again so that you never run out of free food.

GARDEN PEAS

Garden pea

There are lots of different types of peas that can be grown, but the common garden pea is one of the easiest. They taste lovely and sweet, and if you end up with a glut, they are easy to freeze.

Sowing
Grow in well-drained soil in full sun. Add plenty of organic matter before planting. Sow directly in a wide, flat-bottomed trench at about 5cm (2in) deep, in a zigzag pattern 8cm (3in) apart. You can get them started by filling a gutter with compost, sowing the peas and then, when established, sliding the entire section out into the flowerbed.

Growing and care
Peas usually grow to 60cm (24in) high, so provide them with twiggy sticks every 12cm (5in) along a row to keep the plants upright. Alternatively, use pea netting or bamboo and strings. Keep the plants watered during dry periods. Harvest regularly once the peas feel swollen inside the pod, and shell them.

Propagation
Leave a few of the pods on the plant until you can hear the peas rattling inside. Then pick the peas, allow them to dry fully and place them in an envelope or dry storage box. Sow either in autumn under cover or the following spring directly in the soil.

CORN ON
THE COB

Sweetcorn

There is nothing quite as rewarding as corn on the cob picked fresh from the garden. Easy to grow, fresh, homegrown cobs taste so much sweeter than ones from the shops. As well as the usual yellow, there are some other brightly coloured corns to try too, including types for making popcorn.

Sowing

Sweetcorn is slightly tender so should not be planted or sown outdoors until the risk of frost is over. The easiest method is to sow individual seeds into 9cm (3½in) pots under cover from early to mid-May, then plant them outside a few weeks later. Sweetcorn is wind pollinated so should be grown in grids or blocks (see page 14) as opposed to straight rows. They require full sun and fertile yet well-drained soil. Avoid windy sites.

Growing and care

Some of the taller varieties may need staking to keep them upright. Keep a lookout for rodents, squirrels and badgers, which love sweetcorn as much as humans. To tell if the corn is ready, peel back the sheath and stick your thumb into a kernel. If it exudes a milky sap, it's ready. If watery, keep on the plant for longer.

Propagation

To collect the seed for sowing the following year, leave some of the cobs on the plant to ripen fully. Remember that F1 varieties will not come true from seed (see page 58). Also, if you have grown a few different varieties, they may have cross-pollinated and the resulting seedlings will have some variations. Store seeds in a dry, cool place over winter, and sow in late spring the following year in 9cm (3½in) pots.

THREE TO TRY

'Swift' – delicious, ultra-sweet variety with tender kernels; a prolific and reliable cropper. Ripens earlier than most other varieties.

'Mirai Bicolour' – produces an intriguing combination of white and yellow kernels.

'Conqueror' – late-ripening F1 variety that should reward you with at least three cobs per plant.

SWEETCORN KERNELS

RUNNER BEANS

Runner bean

Originally introduced as ornamental plants because of their flowers, runner beans produce delicious pods from midsummer to early autumn.

Sowing

Plant in full sun in fertile, well-drained soil, after the risk of frost is over. Sow in pots or modules indoors to avoid any risk of late frosts or directly in the ground where they are going to be grown. Most are climbing plants, although there are a few dwarf varieties, so will need a support structure such as a wigwam constructed from hazel rods or bamboo canes. Place plants at the base of each bamboo cane at 10cm (4in) apart and tied up to it. Pick beans regularly to keep the plant producing and to prevent stringiness.

FLOWER

Propagation

Harvest pods in late summer and leave them to dry, before storing somewhere cool and dark indoors. Sow the seeds the following spring.

BEAN DEVELOPING

Onion

One of the essential vegetables for any cook, onions can be grown from seed, but most gardeners prefer to grow them initially from sets, bought online or from nurseries. Once you have them in your garden, you can grow from seed.

Planting

Plant in well-drained soil in a sunny position.

Propagation

Onions are ready to harvest once their stems turn brown and start to flop over. If storing onions, dry them in sunshine for a few days beforehand. Flowers might not appear until the second year: if collecting seeds, allow the plant to flower and the seeds to ripen. Remove the seed head and place it in a paper bag. Give it a good shake to remove the seeds, storing them in an envelope somewhere dry and cool indoors. Sow under cover in late winter or early spring. Plant out seedlings a few weeks later in a sunny location in well-drained soil.

SEED HEAD

SEEDS

BEETROOT SEED

Beetroot

This versatile vegetable can be grown as baby beetroots or to full size, with young leaves that are tasty cooked or in salads. Their roots come in a range of colours.

Sowing

Seeds should be sown from April onwards, 1cm (½in) deep and 10cm (4in) apart. If growing more than one row, make the gap 30cm (12in) between them. Sow every few weeks to get a succession of beetroots. Young plants can be harvested when the size of a small ping-pong ball, but they can be left to mature to the size of a cricket ball.

Propagation

Beetroot can be biennial, so you may have to wait until the following season to collect any seed. Leave the flowers to ripen then remove them and leave to dry for two weeks before stripping the dried seed from the spike. Place in an envelope in a dry, cool place indoors and sow from April onwards the following year.

Carrot

CARROT SEED

You might be surprised to discover that carrots are not just orange, but can be purple, black and yellow as well.

Sowing

Carrots need a light or sandy soil. If you have heavy soil, sow in deep pots to allow for the extending root (short or round carrots can be sown in shallower pots), with a seed or potting compost. Seeds are very small, so mix with sand when sowing into shallow drills. Once the carrots germinate, thin them out: 5cm (2in) apart for sweet, baby carrots; up to 15cm (6in) apart for something larger. Seeds can be sown from April onwards, and a succession of sowing every couple of weeks should ensure you always have something to harvest.

Propagation

It may be necessary to wait until the following year before flowers and seeds develop for collecting. If you wish to collect the seed for the following year, leave some plants in the ground and allow the flower to go to seed. Collect in a paper bag and store somewhere dark and cool indoors until the following spring.

Basil *Ocimum basilicum*

If you love Italian cuisine, this aromatic leafy herb is a must-grow either in your garden or on your kitchen windowsill. It needs to be sown regularly to ensure you always have a handful of leaves. There is a range of leaf colours and flavours.

Sowing and planting

Sow seeds indoors from midwinter to midsummer. Sprinkle them lightly over seed compost in 7.5cm (3in) pots or a seed tray. Cover with a layer of vermiculite or grit and place in a propagator or on a warm, sunny windowsill. You can pop a plastic bag over the top of the pots, secured with an elastic band, to act as a mini-greenhouse.

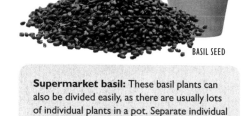

BASIL SEED

Supermarket basil: These basil plants can also be divided easily, as there are usually lots of individual plants in a pot. Separate individual plants and grow them on individually, keep well watered and ensure they continue to receive plenty of warmth and light.

Growing and care

Once the seeds are a few centimetres high and have formed their true leaves, remove them from the propagator, carefully prick out individually and replant into individual 7.5 or 9cm (3 or 3½in) pots. Place them on a warm, sunny windowsill and keep well watered. They can be moved outside, but only when the weather is warm. Once they are about 15cm (6in) high, start harvesting some leaves.

Propagation

To grow for the following year, allow plants to go to seed at the end of summer. Collect the seed heads in a bag and allow to dry out, before storing somewhere cool and dark indoors until starting the sowing sequence again in early winter.

THREE TO TRY

var. *purpurascens* 'Purple Ruffles' – purple ruffle-edged leaves and pretty pink flowers. Wonderful for adding colour to a salad.

Ocimum × *africanum* 'Siam Queen' – ideal for Thai and Southeast Asian cooking, this large-leaved variety has a dark colour and a strong flavour.

'Mrs Burns' Lemon' – delicious and aromatic lemon-flavoured basil.

Parsley *Petroselinum crispum*

Parsley's aromatic leaves are ideal for adding flavour to a range of savoury dishes. Technically, parsley is a biennial, but most people grow it like an annual and sow seeds each year, because the leaves can become a bit tough and tired in their second year. There are two different types: the milder, curly-leaved parsley is more decorative whilst the flat-leaved version packs more of a flavour punch.

Planting and sowing

Best grown in full sun, parsley will cope with partial shade too. Sow seeds outside directly into 1cm (½in) deep drills where you intend to grow them between early spring and early summer. Germination can take up to a few weeks, so be patient. Once they are large enough to handle, thin them out to 15cm (6in) apart between each plant and between other rows. Alternatively, sprinkle some seed into a 9cm (3½in) pot and thin out to just one plant when large enough to handle.

Growing and care

Parsley needs to be kept well watered as it grows, as the leaves will yellow if they dry out. It might be necessary to give them a natural liquid feed every couple of weeks such as nettle or comfrey feed. Regularly harvest the aromatic leaves once they are established in the ground. If you use parsley often in the kitchen, sow every few weeks for a regular supply through summer and into autumn.

Propagation

Remember, parsley is a biennial, so will flower and produce seed in the second year. To collect seed, leave a few plants in the ground to overwinter after the first growing season. Collect the seed once they have ripened, store in a cool, dry place over winter and sow the following spring.

THREE TO TRY

'Bravour' – one of the best curly leaved varieties, with dark foliage and traditional parsley flavour.

'French' – one of the two classic varieties of flat-leaved parsley, 'French' is shorter than the Italian version, growing to 45cm (18in).

'Italian Giant' – the other popular flat-leaved parsley, with more leaves than 'French'. Popular with chefs for a regular supply in the kitchen.

TREES FROM SEEDS AND NUTS

Trees and shrubs can be grown from seed easily, although some may need a cold spell (stratification) before germinating. Other than that, it is just as easy to grow a giant tree as it is to grow a tiny plant, although naturally it can take a lot longer, and many can be grown in containers to restrict their size.

Hazel *Corylus avellana*

Hazel trees are attractive deciduous shrubs with tasty nuts in late summer and autumn, and attractive round leaves and yellow male catkins in spring.

Sowing
Hazel trees will produce more nuts if given plenty of sunlight. Prepare the ground by removing any weeds. They prefer a well-drained soil.

Growing and care
In addition to their ornamental value, hazel can be cut low to the ground in autumn (coppicing) and the fresh young shoots used for weaving fences or making wigwams and climbing structures. Do this every two or three years, or plant more than one hazel, cutting one each year for a steady supply.

Propagation
Hazel can be grown by layering a stem in spring (see page 106) or from seed. To do the latter, harvest the nuts in autumn.

They require stratification, so place in the fridge for a few weeks or grow directly outside. An indication that the seed is ripe is that it is easy to remove from the husk or has fallen to the ground. Check the seed is viable by popping it in water. If it sinks, it is good to use. Place viable seeds individually into potting compost and place outside over winter. You should see signs of growth in early spring.

Hawthorn *Crataegus monogyna*

HAWTHORN BERRIES

Producing fragrant white flowers in late spring, then bright red berries later in the year, hawthorns are very hardy, making them suitable for exposed sites and using as hedge windbreaks. They are one of the best deciduous small trees or shrubs for a small garden and will have a huge benefit for wildlife as well as for yourself.

Sowing
The best way to grow hawthorn is from seed. A seed must go through a period of stratification to break its natural inhibitors that prevents it germinating when it falls naturally in autumn, allowing it to germinate in spring when the conditions are more favourable to grow successfully.

Propagation
Place the seeds into a plastic bag and mix them with a handful of compost. Leave in the fridge for a few weeks before sowing into pots and planting out a few weeks later.

Horse chestnut *Aesculus hippocastanum*

SEED CAPSULES

CONKER SEEDS

Synonymous with autumnal conker fights, these trees with large, conical-shaped spring flowers and hand-shaped foliage are a nostalgic favourite for many of us.

Propagation
Gather the spiky seed cases in autumn from the floor beneath the tree. Remove the conker from its case, mix it with compost and place it in a fridge to stratify it. A few weeks later it can be planted in a pot filled with potting compost and grown on. Alternatively, plant directly into pots in autumn and leave outside, as the cold winter weather is the natural stratification process it would go through in the wild.

FIERY LEAVES OF
THE JAPANESE MAPLE

Japanese maple *Acer palmatum*

One of the most spectacular trees due to its range of palmate-shaped foliage, maples come into their own in autumn, with impressive colours of gold, red, purple and copper. They vary in height from 1 to 20m (3 to 66ft).

Planting

Most are suitable for growing in a container. They prefer dappled shade and moist but well-drained soil, ranging between neutral and slightly acidic, and need to be in a sheltered position.

Propagation

Harvest the seeds when they are falling off the tree and the winged seeds have turned a dark colour. Snap off the wings and soak the seeds in warm water for a few days. Seeds then need stratifying by being placed in a fridge for a few weeks, before being sown in individual pots. If you live in an area with cold winters, plant the seeds directly into pots and leave outside in autumn, as this mimics the cold conditions needed to get an acer growing.

WINGED SEEDS

Oak *Quercus robur*

The majestic English Oak can live for hundreds of years and has huge, thick boughs and attractive-shaped leaves. A single oak tree supports a huge amount of biodiversity.

Propagation

One other familiar feature of the tree is the acorn, and it is from this tiny seed that these mighty trees grow. Acorns can be found on the ground in autumn, beneath the trees. Collect a few and place them in a jar of water: the viable ones will sink. Place them in a fridge for a few weeks after drying to mimic the cold winter they need to break dormancy, then plant them individually in pots and wait for them to germinate.

ACORNS

THE RECOGNISABLE
SHAPE OF THE OAK LEAF

Almond tree *Prunus dulcis*

Almond trees produce attractive white or pink blossom in spring followed by green oval-shaped fruits containing delicious nuts in late summer. They can be grown in containers or as a fan on a south-facing wall. In sheltered, mild gardens they can be grown as an attractive, free-standing tree.

Planting

Almonds flower early and so will need a sheltered spot where the early blossom will not be destroyed by frost. They require full sun in fertile, well-drained soil. If growing as a fan on a south-facing wall or fence, they will need a series of horizontal wires to tie the shoots onto, every 20cm (8in) starting at a height of 40cm–2m (16in–6½ft).

Growing and care

Almonds produce their crop on wood produced the previous year. Avoid pruning the trees in winter as this can cause diseases to enter the plant. Instead, prune when it comes into growth between mid-spring and midsummer. Remove some of the older shoots each year, and tie in new growth that will produce the crop the following year.

Propagation

Shop-bought almond trees are grafted onto a rootstock, so seeds collected from garden varieties will not come true from seed, but it is fun growing them and you might get a new variety. Remove the almond from the green casing and soak it in water for 24 hours to soften the shell. Use a nutcracker to crack the shell, but keep the shell on. Stratify the seeds by placing them in an airtight bag in compost and placing it in the fridge for a few weeks. Plant into individual pots and, when established, plant into a sheltered place in your garden.

ALMOND SEED ENCASED
IN HARD SHELL

THREE TO TRY

'Macrocarpa' – dark leaves and bowl-shaped pale pink flowers followed by large, edible almonds.

'Ingrid' – one of the most hardy almonds, with reliable crops and some resistance to the disease peach leaf curl.

'Robijn' – delicious, sweet-tasting almonds and pinkish-white flowers; partial frost and leaf-curl resistance.

CHAPTER 4

TAKING CUTTINGS

Taking a cutting is an easy way to get an identical plant to the one you've taken it from. It can be done with most trees, shrubs and herbaceous plants, and you can take cuttings of one sort or another at any time of the year, usually from stems but sometimes from roots. You can also reproduce plants by digging up suckers or encouraging their lower branches to layer on the ground and produce roots. If you use a range of these techniques your garden will soon fill up with lots of your favourite plants.

In this chapter you will find step-by-step guides on how to take both hardwood and softwood cuttings. There are also tips on how to layer a shrub to produce more plants, as well as how to dig up a sucker and grow it on. There are plant profiles for some of the most suitable plants on which to try these techniques. You will also find information on troubleshooting and discover useful tips on how and where to look after your cuttings. Finally, there is some advice on how to use hormone rooting powder, to encourage cuttings to 'take' and maximise your success rate.

CUTTINGS BASICS

If you've had your envious eye on a friend or neighbour's plant, then one of the simplest ways of getting your own one for free is to ask if you can take a cutting. It does not have to be a garden plant, either. Even out in the countryside, cuttings of plants such as blackberries or elderflower are easy to take, assuming you have asked permission from the landowner, of course.

Taking cuttings couldn't be simpler and does not require any specialist equipment. From one plant you can get lots and lots of freebie plants. All you need is a pair of secateurs, a bag and some compost. For some trickier plants you may need some hormone rooting powder to encourage roots to grow, but most will take without any.

WHAT IS A CUTTING?

It is simply a small section of the original plant that is removed and placed into compost. This 'cutting' should then develop its own set of roots and become a new plant. Cuttings are usually taken from healthy, new growth and vary in size from about 5 to 20cm (2½ to 8in).

The average length of a cutting is 8–15cm (3–6in), which is already established with a stem and leaves.

WHY TAKE A CUTTING?

A cutting is like cloning the original plant. If you want the same plant, with all those characteristics, such as growth habit, colour of flower, height and scent, then a cutting is the best way to achieve this. It should result in a practically identical plant to the one the cutting has been taken from.

Unlike growing plants from seed, which show variation in characteristics, plants from cuttings will be identical to their parents. This is definitely an advantage if you see a plant in someone else's garden and you want exactly the same thing in your garden, with exactly the same colour flowers or leaves.

Another advantage of taking cuttings is that they are quicker to establish than growing from seed.

Many gardeners enjoy the challenge of taking cuttings, and there is enormous satisfaction and wonder in getting a favourite plant to produce lots of offspring from just a few offcuts, which can then be shared with friends.

IT'S ALL ABOUT TIMING

Cuttings can be taken all year round, depending on the type of cutting you are taking.

- **Hardwood cuttings** – mid-autumn to early spring.
- **Softwood cuttings** – spring to early summer.
- **Greenwood cuttings** – early to midsummer.
- **Semi-ripe cuttings** – midsummer to mid-autumn.

WHAT CUTTINGS NEED

It is possible to bring cuttings on with very little in the way of specialist equipment, and for anyone just starting out there is a benefit to keeping things simple. The fundamentals include a place to grow your cuttings, good hygiene, and the right temperature, moisture and light levels. With the basics mastered, you may enjoy the challenge of taking material from plants that are more difficult to propagate.

WHERE TO GROW

Some cuttings can be put directly into the ground in the garden. This is usually the case for hardy hardwood cuttings, such as a gooseberry or a flowering currant. They can be left outside over winter and then carefully dug up in late summer, when they have established roots, and individually planted in their final position.

Less-hardy plants will require a humid condition because they do not have any roots to supply them with liquid. This is usually cuttings with foliage, such as soft and semi-ripe cuttings, as they need moisture to sustain them. They are also actively growing at the time the cutting is taken.

LET THERE BE LIGHT

Just like established plants, most cuttings require some light to grow successfully. However, most cuttings will struggle if placed in direct sunlight, particularly if on a sunny windowsill or in a greenhouse where the glass can intensify the sun's rays. This can cause emerging shoots or leaves to scorch and the compost to dry out quickly. Also avoid deep shade, which is the other extreme. Diffused or soft indirect light provides the ideal growing conditions for most cuttings.

TEMPERATURE-CONTROLLED
PROPAGATOR

Apart from hardy hardwood ones, cuttings should be kept in a frost-free environment.

GIVE CUTTINGS A HELPING HAND

Troubleshooting

Always research the most suitable time to propagate a plant. Some plants are more successful from hardwood or softwood cuttings.

Some may require a heel or the use of hormone rooting powder. And don't forget, some cuttings require warmth for them to 'take' or 'strike' (produce roots). Finally, check on the moisture levels.

IF OVERWATERED, YOUR CUTTINGS COULD ROT, BUT IF UNDERWATERED, THEY COULD DRY OUT.

Keeping less-hardy plants moist

To provide extra moisture, cuttings can either be placed in a propagator or have a plastic bag placed over the pot, held in place with an elastic band.

CUT AWAY THE BOTTOM OF A PLASTIC BOTTLE AND USE THE TOP SECTION AS A CLOCHE TO PROVIDE EXTRA MOISTURE AND WARMTH.

HORMONE ROOTING POWDER

Some cuttings require a little 'persuasion' when trying to get them to strike. Gardeners often use a product called hormone rooting powder to stimulate root growth. It is also possible to buy it in gel or liquid form. The base of the cutting is dipped in it before being inserted into the compost or soil. It consists of a synthetic auxin, which replicates the natural hormone found in plants used to stimulate plant growth. Hormone rooting powder also contains fungicide.

There are also organic hormone rooting powders that contain the natural auxin plant hormone instead of synthetic versions. Seek these out if you are an organic gardener.

Some gels and liquids may need diluting, so check the label before using. Avoid getting it on other parts of the plant such as green shoots and leaves as this can damage it.

PLANTS THAT NEED ASSISTANCE

Some plants that nearly always need assistance with hormone rooting powder (gel) include:

- Citrus
- Dahlia
- Fuchsia
- Hibiscus
- Lobelia
- Osteospermum
- Salvia
- Snapdragon

PLANTS THAT CAN GO IT ALONE

Not all plants require hormone rooting powder. These include:

- Most succulents
- Rosemary
- Mint
- Hydrangea
- Petunia
- Lavender
- Perennial wallflower

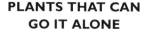

LAVENDER

SUCCULENT

SALVIA

HOW TO USE ROOTING POWDER (OR LIQUID/GEL)

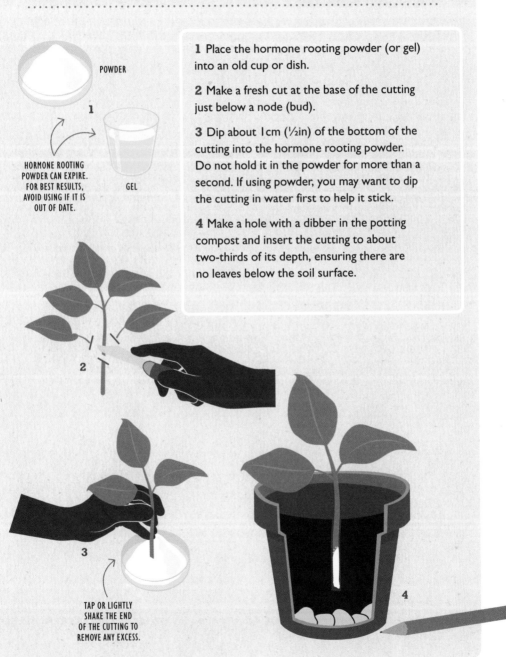

POWDER

GEL

HORMONE ROOTING
POWDER CAN EXPIRE.
FOR BEST RESULTS,
AVOID USING IF IT IS
OUT OF DATE.

1 Place the hormone rooting powder (or gel) into an old cup or dish.

2 Make a fresh cut at the base of the cutting just below a node (bud).

3 Dip about 1cm (½in) of the bottom of the cutting into the hormone rooting powder. Do not hold it in the powder for more than a second. If using powder, you may want to dip the cutting in water first to help it stick.

4 Make a hole with a dibber in the potting compost and insert the cutting to about two-thirds of its depth, ensuring there are no leaves below the soil surface.

TAP OR LIGHTLY
SHAKE THE END
OF THE CUTTING TO
REMOVE ANY EXCESS.

SOFTWOOD AND GREENWOOD CUTTINGS

Softwood cuttings are taken as the plant comes into growth in spring using the soft new stems. It is an easy method of propagating as the rapid new growth roots quickly. But the cuttings are quick to dry out and die, so they will need the protection of a controlled environment to make sure they survive until new roots have formed. Softwood cuttings can be taken from deciduous shrubs and herbaceous perennials. A few trees and shrubs can also be propagated this way.

Collect the soft stems on the day you are going to propagate them, looking for fresh new growth that is healthy and free from pest and disease. Avoid flowering stems but instead look for 'vegetative' growth.

Young vs old: Younger plants are usually more vigorous, produce more healthy, fresh growth and are therefore easier to propagate. If you wish to propagate an older plant, it is worth cutting back hard a few months beforehand to stimulate new vigorous growth.

GREENWOOD CUTTINGS ARE SIMILAR TO SOFTWOOD ONES BUT ARE TAKEN LATER IN THE SEASON (EARLY SUMMER) WHEN THE BASE OF THE NEW GROWTH IS NOT AS SOFT. USE THE SAME TECHNIQUE AS FOR SOFTWOOD CUTTINGS, JUST MAKE THE CUTTING SLIGHTLY LONGER, 10–12CM (4–5IN).

HOW TO TAKE SOFTWOOD AND GREENWOOD CUTTINGS

You will need:
- Secateurs
- Deciduous plant or herbaceous perennial
- Plastic bags
- Fridge, if not able to put the cuttings in compost immediately
- Sharp knife
- Hormone rooting powder (optional)
- Cutting compost
- 9cm (3½in) pots or modules
- Dibber, pencil or stick
- Watering can
- Propagator (optional)

1 Cut about 10cm (4in) of the fresh shoot, including the tip. Cut just above a bud on the mother plant.

2 Place the softwood stem in a plastic bag whilst collecting others. If you are not going to propagate immediately, place the cutting in the fridge.

3 Pinch out the growing tip of the cutting.

4 Lay out the cutting on a table and use a sharp knife to cut the base of the cutting just below a node (bud). This area is most likely to produce roots.

5 Remove two-thirds of the lower leaves with secateurs or by stripping them off between your thumb and index finger.

6 Place the base of the stem in hormone rooting powder if it is the type of plant that does not readily strike.

7 Fill a 9cm (3½in) pot with cutting compost and use a dibber, pencil or blunt stick to make a hole. Carefully insert the cutting into the hole and firm the soil back around the cutting.

8 Water the cutting and place in a sheltered, light position out of direct sunlight.

9 A propagator is ideal, or a plastic transparent bag can be placed over the pot and secured with an elastic band to help retain moisture.

10 The cuttings will take three or four weeks to root. Then gradually harden them off (see page 62) until they can tolerate being planted outside permanently (assuming the plants are fully hardy and not houseplants or tender exotics).

TO INCREASE SUCCESS RATES, TAKE LOTS OF CUTTINGS AND INSERT IN THE SAME POT.

7

SEMI-RIPE CUTTINGS

Semi-ripe cuttings are taken towards the end of summer and into mid-autumn. It is the time when a young stem has started to ripen at the base and transform into wood but still has soft green growth at the top. It's a useful time of year to get out into the garden, take stock of the plants you enjoyed over the summer and collect new cuttings for the following year.

The technique for taking a semi-ripe cutting is similar to taking a softwood cutting (see page 92). Apart from the timing, the main difference is that semi-ripe cuttings are usually slightly longer than softwood cuttings, at about 12cm (5in) in length. The base should be brown and turning woody, whilst the other end should be much greener and softer.

One of the benefits of taking a semi-ripe cutting as opposed to softwood ones is that the stem is less likely to wilt and dehydrate as it has developed a more rigid, sturdy and

sustainable structure. It is a technique used on lots of shrubs including *Choisya*, *Hebe*, *Penstemon*, *Viburnum*, and some culinary herbs like rosemary and sage.

Large-leaved plants: To reduce water loss in cuttings of these types of plants, cut the leaves in half with a clean, sharp knife.

Rosemary is an easy shrub to propagate from semi-ripe cuttings taken in late summer or early autumn.

VARIATIONS

In addition to taking a traditional semi-ripe cutting, there are a couple of slight variations known as heel cuttings and wounding.

Heel cuttings

Some shrubs such as *Berberis, Camellia, Cotinus, Lonicera* and *Jasminum* strike better if they are removed just near the base of the older wood, retaining a small tail or 'heel' of the bark from the older material when removed. This 'heel' is dipped in hormone rooting powder before being placed in compost.

1 To remove a cutting with a heel, use secateurs to cut most of the way through the stem where you are taking the cutting from.

2 Then pull downwards, which should detach the stem from the mother plant and rip a 'tail' of bark with it. If the tail is too long it can be trimmed to about 1cm (½in) long.

Wounding

Some woody plants (trees and shrubs) are easier to propagate if they are 'wounded' first.

1 Use a sharp knife to scrape away 1–2cm (½–¾in) at the base of the outer layer of the cutting.

2 Dip the base in hormone rooting powder to encourage it to send out roots.

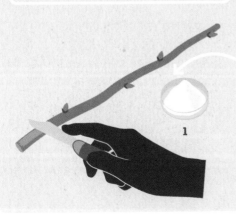

TAKING A HARDWOOD CUTTING

Hardwood cuttings are easily taken when the plant is dormant; the best time is at leaf fall – run your fingers down the stem and if the leaves come away easily then it is time. They require no specialist propagation skills or equipment. This technique suits plants that produce woody stems, such as deciduous plants (the ones that go dormant). Some examples are willow, dogwoods, gooseberries and redcurrants, roses and elderflower.

EVERGREEN

Evergreen cuttings still have foliage during the dormant season, so will need extra protection from water loss. Place a bag over the pot to retain humidity, or keep cuttings in a propagator with a lid. Add leaf mould to the potting mix as another way to help retain moisture.

> Take hardwood cuttings when the plant is dormant – avoid taking them in extreme cold or frost as this can damage the woody material.

HELPING HARDY HARDWOOD CUTTINGS

When taking a few cuttings like this, it can help to dig out a shallow trench and insert a row or line of cuttings at two-thirds their depth, before backfilling the trench and firming them in. Distance each cutting at about a hand-width apart, as this will give each one enough space to develop roots and shoots.

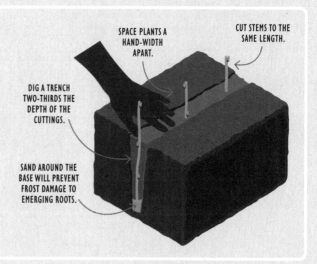

SPACE PLANTS A HAND-WIDTH APART.

CUT STEMS TO THE SAME LENGTH.

DIG A TRENCH TWO-THIRDS THE DEPTH OF THE CUTTINGS.

SAND AROUND THE BASE WILL PREVENT FROST DAMAGE TO EMERGING ROOTS.

TAKING A HARDWOOD CUTTING

You will need:
- Secateurs
- Woody plant
- Pot
- General purpose, peat-free compost (or the cuttings can be inserted directly into the soil as on page 88)

Be patient: Wait for the cutting to root properly before transplanting it.

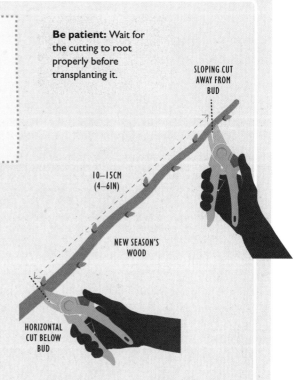

SLOPING CUT AWAY FROM BUD

10–15CM (4–6IN)

NEW SEASON'S WOOD

HORIZONTAL CUT BELOW BUD

1 Remove 10–15cm (4–6in) of healthy, new woody stems with a pair of secateurs. Check the plant material is healthy by looking for any abnormalities on the stems.

2 Use the secateurs to remove the softer material at the tip, making the cut just above a bud and angled away from it. This should ensure that the rain will not run onto it and cause rot.

3 Cut the base of the cutting to just below a bud. Sometimes it can help to lightly scratch the surface of the woody stem near the base to encourage the stem to send out roots.

Safe storage: If you are not able to plant your hardwood cuttings directly into compost or soil immediately, place them in a plastic bag and store in the fridge. Plant them into soil before spring.

4 Push the hardwood cutting about two-thirds of its length into the compost. Place them about 5cm (2in) apart around the edge of the pot. You should be able to fit a few in.

5 You will begin to see new growth in spring as the cutting emerges from its dormancy. Keep the compost moist during its first spring/summer while the new root system establishes itself.

Elderflower *Sambucus nigra*

The elderflower bush is popular in the garden, with some varieties providing pretty, variegated or serrated foliage. There are also purple-leaved varieties with showy pink flowers instead of the traditional white.

Propagation

Remove young healthy growth once leaves drop off the tree in autumn. Use secateurs to trim the bottom of the shoot to just below a bud. Cut the top so that it is about 10–15cm (4–6in) long. Insert the lower two-thirds into soil or compost. Elderberries are hardy, so the hardwood cuttings can be grown outside either in a container or in the soil.

Planting

Keep the cuttings well watered and out of direct sunlight. The following autumn, it should be possible to carefully lift the individual cuttings out of the soil/compost and plant them out in the garden, or pot them on individually into containers. They prefer full sun or dappled shade and can grow to about 3m (10ft) tall and can be just as wide.

Maintenance and picking

Elderflower bushes require little maintenance but can have a sprawling habit, so trim back branches in winter if unwieldy. In spring, their delicate, scented white flowers can be picked. Harvest them on a sunny day when the golden pollen can be seen on the surface of the flower. This will ensure the best flavours if making cordial or sparkling wine. Berries should be picked when they turn black and juicy, or when the birds start to eat them!

THREE TO TRY

'**Black Beauty**' – dark purple, almost black foliage followed by bright pinkish-purple flowers.

'**Black Lace**' – similar flowers and berries to 'Black Beauty' but has finely cut, purple foliage.

'**Golden Tower**' – finely divided, bright golden foliage with a compact habit; ideal for a small space.

Rosemary *Salvia rosmarinus*

This popular evergreen shrub not only smells good but looks great too. It has dark green, needle-like foliage and in spring has attractive blue, star-shaped flowers. Whichever variety you choose, you will have an endless supply of seasoning to use in the kitchen.

Propagation

Although rosemary can be grown from seed, it is much quicker and easier to take cuttings. Softwood cuttings are best taken in spring, just as the plant starts to make new growth. Remove 12cm (5in) lengths of healthy new growth with secateurs. Rub off the lowest two-thirds of the needles by running the stem between your fingers and thumb. Insert two-thirds of the cutting into a gritty or well-drained compost.

Planting

A few months later the rosemary cuttings should be ready for planting out in the garden. They are frost-hardy so can tolerate cold weather, but they hate being in waterlogged soil, so make sure they are planted in well-drained conditions. If you have heavy soil, add plenty of grit to improve the drainage. They are also suitable for growing in containers for evergreen interest. The upright variety can be planted as a formal hedge if planted in a line at 40cm (16in) spacing.

Maintenance and picking

Each year, cut back rosemary lightly after flowering to prevent it getting too straggly. Sprigs can be picked all year round, but they are at their most aromatic in late spring and summer when the sun has encouraged them to produce an abundance of their essential oils that give off their distinct fragrance.

THREE TO TRY

'Miss Jessopp's Upright' – upright stems make it suitable for hedging or formal gardens.

'Majorca Pink' – another upright variety, with attractive pink flowers.

Prostrata Group – lax (non-upright) habit, making it suitable for ground cover or planting in informal borders or rock gardens. Popular varieties include 'Capri' and 'Rampant Boule'.

ROOT CUTTINGS

Some plants are easier to propagate from root cuttings than from hard or softwood cuttings. Ideally, these are plants that naturally sucker and send up shoots when growing in the garden. It is often done with herbaceous perennials, although it can work with some shrubs and trees too.

WOOD ANEMONE

NEW ROOTS GROWING

NEW SHOOT

PLANTS TO TRY

- *Acanthus mollis* (bear's breech)
- *Ailanthus*
- *Anemone* × *hybrida* (Japanese anemone)
- *Aralia*
- *Campsis*
- *Catalpa* (Indian bean tree)
- *Chaenomeles* (Japanese quince)
- *Clerodendrum*
- *Echinops* (globe thistle)
- *Mentha* (mint)
- *Papaver orientale* (oriental poppy)
- *Passiflora* (passion flower)
- *Phlox*
- *Primula denticulata* (drumstick primula)
- *Rhus*
- *Robinia*
- *Solanum*
- *Sophora*
- *Syringa* (lilac)
- *Verbascum*

A root cutting is simply the removal of a section of root from the mother plant, grown to make a new plant. Take root cuttings when they are dormant, which is usually from late autumn through to late winter.

Japanese anemones are vigorous herbaceous perennials popular for their late summer flowers. They are easy to grow from root cuttings.

THICK OR FLESHY ROOTS

You will need:
- Plant with roots suitable for root cuttings
- Spade
- Secateurs
- Knife for cutting roots
- 9cm (3½in) pots
- Seed or cutting compost

1 Using a spade, and only in winter or when it is not actively growing, dig up the plant from which you wish to propagate.

2 Wash the roots with water so that you can see the material you need to cut.

3 Use a pair of secateurs to remove a few sections of pencil-thick roots near the crown of the plant.

4 Cut the root into 6cm (2½in) lengths, retaining the thicker part near the crown and discarding the thinner root and fibrous material further down the root.

5 Insert the root cutting vertically into seed or cutting compost. To ensure the plant will root, keep the end nearest the crown at the surface.

6 Be sure that the top of the root cutting is level with the surface of the compost.

7 Plants produce leaves before the roots, so be patient and make sure plants are growing below the surface before transplanting them to individual larger pots.

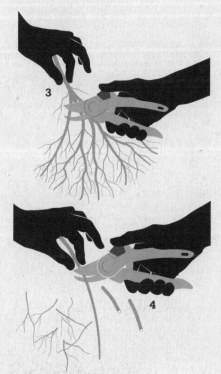

Thinner root systems: Plants such as Japanese anemones, phlox and geraniums will need 8cm (3in) lengths of root placed horizontally on the surface of compost and covered with horticultural grit.

Bear's breech *Acanthus mollis*

Acanthus are beautiful herbaceous perennials producing spikes of white flowers surrounded by purple-coloured bracts. They are easy to grow; in fact some might say too easy, as they like to spread out once established. Their semi-evergreen, dark green, shapely foliage was often the inspiration for patterns of the Arts and Crafts movement.

Planting

These plants like fertile, well-drained soil in full sun, although they will tolerate some shade. They can be bullies in the borders, so will need space to avoid smothering their neighbours. Plant individual plants at 50cm (20in) apart in autumn or early spring. Grow in a pot if you are concerned about spread.

Growing and maintenance

In late winter, cut back the semi-evergreen foliage to near ground level, if it looks untidy. It might be necessary to trim the roots back if they are encroaching on other areas.

Propagation

Acanthus is best propagated by either division or with root cuttings. Lift the rootball in autumn and remove 6cm (2½in) lengths of root that are of pencil thickness. Plant vertically into individual pots, with the part of the plant that was growing nearest the crown nearest the surface. Plant the cutting outside in spring when it has produced shoots that are about 6cm (2½in) high.

THREE TO TRY

Acanthus mollis 'Hollard's Gold' – golden foliage with white flowers and purple, hooded bracts.

Acanthus 'Whitewater' – interesting, white-splashed foliage with creamy coloured flowers surrounded by purple bracts.

Acanthus mollis 'Tasmanian Angel' – dwarf and compact variety, originating from Turkey, with white-splashed foliage.

Globe thistle *Echinops*

Loved by bees, these thistles start flowering from midsummer, but the round flower heads remain held aloft amongst architectural foliage well into autumn.

Planting

These plants require a sunny spot in well-drained soil. They can reach up to 1.5m (5ft) high so plant towards the back of a border. Easy to grow, with little maintenance, when they have finished flowering you can leave for the wildlife to enjoy. Cut down to near ground level in late winter or early spring.

Propagation

Either divide in autumn or grow from fleshy root cuttings in winter. To do this, remove 6–8cm (2½–3in) lengths of root near the crown and insert vertically into pots in well-drained compost, ensuring the part closest to the crown is at the top. Plant cuttings out in the garden in spring once they have grown their own root system.

Indian bean tree *Catalpa bignonioides*

This deciduous ornamental tree produces huge leaves and large showy flowers in summer, and later provides an impressive display of slender seed pods.

Planting

Add organic matter and plant in a sheltered sunny position. If growing as a freestanding tree, leave space around it; at the back of a border prune hard annually to keep compact. In late winter or early spring use loppers to cut back new growth to 50cm (20in) above the ground. This will encourage young shoots, to grow into a multi-stemmed tree.

Propagation

Catalpa can be propagated by seed or softwood cuttings. Another technique is to take root cuttings in autumn. Dig around the base of the tree and remove 10cm (4in) lengths of finger-thick roots. Insert vertically into well-drained compost with the top being the section that was closest to the trunk.

LEAF CUTTINGS

Another section of a plant that you can use to propagate from are the leaves. It is a technique often used, although not exclusively, to propagate houseplants. As the name suggests, it simply involves removing a leaf from the plant and using it to produce lots more. Sometimes it requires the whole leaf, and other times just sections of it.

The best time to take leaf cuttings is when they are actively growing, which is usually between spring and midsummer.

LEAF CUTTING

NEW PLANT

PROPAGATE USING PART OF A LEAF

This is one of the most popular techniques, used to grow new *Streptocarpus* (Cape primrose) plants.

1 Remove a healthy, young leaf from the plant you wish to propagate.

2 Use a knife to carefully cut down the central midrib so that it is in two sections.

3 Add hormone rooting powder along the edge of the freshly cut leaf.

4 Fill a seed tray with well-drained potting compost and make a 5mm (¼in) deep groove in it. Plant the freshly cut edge into it and firm the compost back around it.

5 Place it in a light, warm place indoors but not in direct sunlight.

6 Keep the cutting watered. After a few weeks tiny leaves will emerge from the edge of the cut leaf in the compost.

PROPAGATE USING A WHOLE LEAF

It is possible to grow plants using a whole leaf. One of the techniques is used for succulents such as *Crassula* (jade plant).

1 Remove a healthy, plump succulent leaf from the main stem.

2 Leave the leaves to dry out and callous over at the wound area for a few days.

3 Place the base of the leaf (now hopefully callused over) into pot filled with a well-drained cutting compost.

4 Make sure the remainder of the leaf is not in contact with the compost as this can cause it to rot. Use cocktail sticks to hold it aloft if it will not curve away naturally from the compost.

5 Place the cuttings in a light, warm and humid environment. The compost should be kept moist, but not too wet, because this can cause the plant material to rot.

6 A new plantlet should start to form at the base of the leaf after two or three months. It can stay there for another few months until it is established enough to be removed and potted on.

KEEP SOIL MOIST
BUT NOT TOO WET.

LAYERING

This is one of the easiest techniques for propagating your favourite trees and shrubs. The new plant is kept alive by the parent until it is established and can be separated.

Layering does take patience, however, as it can take about 12 months before a new plant is formed and is ready to be planted elsewhere. The best time to layer a plant is in spring, although some deciduous plants will respond well to this technique in autumn too.

SUITABLE PLANTS

There are many suitable plants including:
- *Acer*
- *Camellia*
- *Cornus*
- *Daphne*
- *Forysthia*
- *Magnolia*
- *Rhododendron*

AIR-LAYERING

Use this technique if there are not any suitable flexible branches that will stretch to the ground.

1 Choose a healthy, straight section of a mature stem formed the previous year.

2 Remove the leaves for a 30cm (12in) section. In the centre, use a knife to make a 2cm- (1in-) long wound, cutting through a leaf bud.

3 Add hormone rooting powder to the wound.

4 Use tape to wrap a black plastic bag below the wound.

5 Soak sphagnum moss overnight beforehand so that it is thoroughly wet. Pack the bag full of moss then tape up the top end to seal it. In a few months' time, roots will have started to form.

6 Use secateurs to cut the branch just below the root system and plant it somewhere else in the garden.

HOW TO LAYER A BRANCH

You will need:
- Metal peg
- Knife
- Spade
- Secateurs
- Watering can

1 Look for a flexible, low-growing branch on a plant that is long enough to reach down to the ground.

2 Identify the section of the branch that will be in contact with the soil, and use your knife to scrap away a 2 x 2cm (¾ x ¾in) section of the bark to reveal the cambium layer.

3 Dig a hole 8cm (3in) deep where the branch meets the ground and peg the branch into it.

4 Cover this section of the branch over with soil and water it.

5 Make sure that the tip of the shoot is not covered over, but instead comes out the other side of the hole.

6 A year later the plant can be cut from the mother plant with a pair of secateurs.

7 The section of branch that had been layered into the soil should have grown new roots and can be dug up and planted elsewhere in the garden.

PLANTS SUITABLE FOR LAYERING

There are a number of plants that are suitable for layering. You may find some shrubs even do it naturally themselves when they have low branches touching the soil. If not, we can give them a hand by pegging them down into the soil to encourage them to develop roots and become a new plant.

Camellia

This popular evergreen shrub boasts glossy leaves and a display of rose-like flowers in early spring, although there are some species that flower in autumn.

Planting and maintenance

They prefer a slightly acidic soil, so add ericaceous compost to the area when planting if you do not have these conditions. If the soil is too alkaline, grow in large pots using ericaceous potting compost. They do not require much maintenance but can be trimmed after flowering if they need to be tidied up.

Propagation

Camellias lend themselves well to air-layering (see page 106). Simply find a healthy young shoot, strip the leaves off an area of about 30cm (12in) then use a knife to cut a 2cm (¾in) sliver of bark away all around it. Wet the area then dust it with hormone rooting powder. The moisture should help it stick. Wrap a black plastic bag around the area packed full of wet moss and secure each end with tape. In a few months' time it will have produced roots from the wounded area, and this section can be removed with secateurs and planted elsewhere in the garden.

Grape vine *Vitis vinifera*

Grape vines are climbers with attractive lobbed foliage, which produce grapes. Some varieties such as 'Purpurea' and 'Brandt' also produce a colourful autumn foliage display.

Planting and maintenance

As a general rule, dessert grapes should be grown under glass in temperate climates in order to reach optimum sweetness, whereas wine grapes are grown outdoors. They prefer well-drained soil in full sun. They will also need a structure such as a trellis or archway to scramble up with their tendrils.

Propagation

Grape vines can be propagated by hardwood cuttings, but another successful method is serpentine layering. It is similar to standard layering but because vines have such long stems, they can be weaved in and out of the soil to produce numerous new plants all along their length.

Magnolia

With an ancient lineage and impressive flowers, magnolias have both deciduous and evergreen types, with the former producing flowers from late winter through to mid-spring, and the latter flowering in late summer.

Planting and maintenance

They prefer a moist, well-drained soil ranging from neutral to slightly acidic. Some magnolias can grow to become large trees, so make sure they are given plenty of space, although species such as *M. stellata* (star magnolia) are more compact.

Propagation

Magnolias can be grown from seed, but a more effective method, especially if you want to have an exact copy of what you are propagating from, is to air-layer them using the same method as for a camellia (see page 108).

GRAFTING BASICS

Grafting and budding – taking two plants and joining them together so that they make one – are very satisfying techniques to master. They are commonly seen on roses, where a choice variety is grafted onto a strong-growing rootstock to give the grafted plant more vigour.

The words 'budding' and 'grafting' are often used interchangeably in the world of gardening, though grafting involves attaching a stick or shoot (scion) onto another plant, whereas budding involves transferring a single bud onto another one. Grafting usually takes place in late winter or early spring, just as the weather is warming up. Budding is often done from mid- to late summer.

WHY GRAFT OR BUD?

Many plants bought from a nursery or garden centre will have been grafted or budded onto a different set of roots. If you look carefully near the base of a plant such as a wisteria, maple or apple tree you will see a bulge on the stem, just above ground level and that is where the plant has been grafted (or budded).

There are a few reasons for this. Firstly, the variety that you wish to grow might be too big and vigorous on its own roots. By grafting it onto a dwarfing rootstock, it becomes more suitable for a small garden or for growing in a pot.

Another reason for grafting onto rootstocks is to improve your plant's resistance to soil-borne pests and diseases.

Rootstocks are bred especially for their vigour, health and tolerance of adverse environmental conditions.

There are also some plants that do not come true from seed, yet do not readily 'strike' from cuttings either. In this case, grafting provides a solution.

Finally, there are commercial reasons. Farmers may graft a new variety of apple onto existing trees, because the older variety was prone to disease or not very productive.

DID YOU KNOW?

It is usually trees and shrubs that are grafted, but there are even some vegetable plants grown using this technique if you buy them from specialist suppliers. Some of the most common types are tomatoes, chillies and aubergines. They are grafted onto rootstocks to increase vigour and provide protection from some soil-borne viruses or pests.

DIFFERENT GRAFTING TECHNIQUES

There are a few different techniques to grafting or budding, depending on what you wish to achieve. Some of the most common are:

Chip, shield or T-budding

Removing a section from the rootstock and inserting a bud into it.

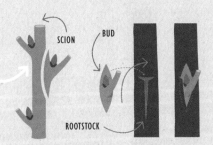

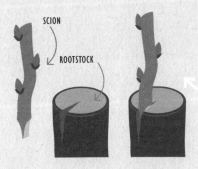

Cleft grafting

Technique used to attach scions to a mature and thicker piece of branch.

Saddle grafting

The rootstock is made into a wedge, and the scion stick is made into a deep cleft at its base which sits on the wedge, like a saddle, then is bound with grafting tape.

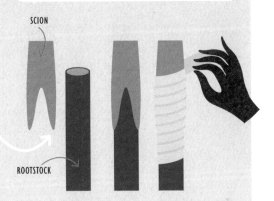

Whip and tongue grafting

See page 113 for this technique.

GRAFTING AN APPLE TREE OR PEAR TREE

Apple and pear trees are grafted onto rootstocks because their own natural root systems are too vigorous. Nursery-bought fruit trees are almost always supplied on named rootstocks, chosen because they will control the eventual size of the tree. Fruit trees do not easily grow from cuttings, or come true from seed. Grafting onto a rootstock enables you to propagate your favourite tree.

Although you can buy grafted trees from specialist fruit nurseries, it is far more rewarding (and cheaper) to buy rootstocks and graft a variety that you may have discovered somewhere. It is also useful if you believe a tree is rare as it is unlikely a fruit nursery will have it in stock. If you have discovered a potentially unique variety then it is even more important that you can graft it, so that it can be conserved.

Grafting takes place from late winter through to early spring as the plant comes out of dormancy. The rootstock and the scion need to be the same species.

Apple trees do not come true from seed, so the best way to propagate a variety is to graft it onto a rootstock.

WHIP AND TONGUE GRAFTING

You will need:
- Rootstock (apple: M26 is a good size, growing to 2.5m/8ft; pear: Quince C will grow to 2.5–3m/8–10ft)
- Apple or pear tree you wish to propagate
- Secateurs
- Spade
- Grafting tape
- Grafting knife or sharp gardening knife

1 Plant your chosen rootstock in the ground in winter, about 12 months before you plan on grafting your chosen variety.

2 Between mid- and late winter, whilst the tree is dormant, select 25cm (10in) pencil-thick lengths of young stems from the tree you wish to propagate from. These will become your 'scion' sticks.

3 Wrap your scion sticks up in a plastic bag and place in the fridge until you are ready for grafting.

4 In February cut down your rootstock to about 25cm (10in) above ground level with secateurs or a pair of loppers. Remove any side-shoots.

5 Use a sharp knife to make a sloping cut at the top of the rootstock.

6 Cut a 5mm (¼in) groove into the sloping cut on the rootstock to form a 'tongue'.

7 Trim the top of the scion stick so that it is about three or four buds long.

8 At the bottom of the scion stick make a sloping cut to correspond with the sloping cut on the rootstock.

9 Cut a 5mm (¼in) downward groove across the face of the angled slope on the scion stick at one-third of the way down to make another 'tongue'.

10 Slot the two tongues into each other so that they entwine and lock.

11 Use grafting tape to bind and tie together the rootstock and scion stick.

12 About two months later the scion and rootstock should have callused over where the two sections have joined and become one plant.

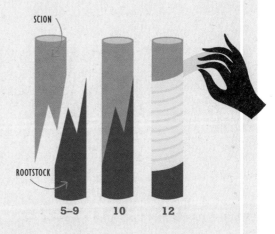

SCION

ROOTSTOCK

5–9   10   12

CHAPTER 5

HOUSEPLANTS

Houseplants, in their vast range of colours, shapes and sizes, can bring the interior of a home to life. Some make large architectural features and focal points in a room, whilst others are small and compact and can easily fit on a shelf in a kitchen or bathroom. Some have trailing habits whilst others are climbers. A few prefer shade and others will love a bright window. Suffice to say, you won't be short of opportunities to grow plants indoors, and reasons to propagate them.

Most houseplants are easy to propagate from seeds, cuttings or division. Some naturally produce offshoots at the base, or miniature 'plantlets' at the end of shoots, which can simply be removed and potted on to become another plant. In this chapter you will find everything you need to know about the basics of propagating houseplants and how to care for them, including how to take stem cuttings in water or compost and propagate from offshoots. There is also a range of plant profiles for you to choose houseplants to suit your home.

HOUSEPLANT PROPAGATION BASICS

There is a vast array of different houseplants that can be grown indoors, including cacti, succulents, climbers, trailing plants and many more. We might not all have a garden, but we probably all have room for a houseplant. Not only do they look good, but they also purify the air and improve our mental well-being.

Thankfully most houseplants are easy to propagate, with various methods of doing it. As well as the usual propagation techniques such as division, seed sowing and cuttings (see also Leaf Cuttings, page 104), there are a few other techniques of gaining more houseplants for free.

TINY BABIES

MOTHER PLANT

EASIEST TO PROPAGATE

Kalanchoe daigremontiana is commonly known as 'mother of thousands' for a good reason. It produces lots of 'babies' all along the edges of its leaves. Propagating could not be simpler. Just carefully remove individual babies from the leaves and pot into individual pots. Alternatively, you can simply place a pot of compost under the mother plant and leave it for a few weeks. It is guaranteed that baby plants will have dropped into the compost and established themselves in the pot.

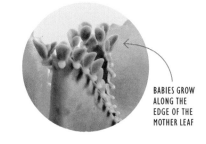

BABIES GROW ALONG THE EDGE OF THE MOTHER LEAF

CUTTINGS IN WATER

One of the easiest methods of propagating a houseplant is to take a cutting and get it to root in water instead of compost.

1 Take 10–20cm (4–8in) lengths of healthy stems from the plant you wish to propagate.

2 Use a knife to cut just below a bud, and strip off the lower leaves so that they do not sit and rot in the water.

3 Fill a jar or pot with water and place the stem in it, ensuring the leaves are not submerged.

4 In a few weeks' time you will notice that the base of the stems have produced roots.

5 These rooted stems can be planted into compost and grown as new houseplants.

2

3

SUITABLE PLANTS

Plants for growing cuttings in water include:
- Missionary plant, *Pilea peperomioides*
- Basil, *Ocimum basilicum*
- *Coleus*
- *Impatiens*
- Heart-leaf philodendron, *Philodendron scandens*
- Pothos, *Epipremnum aureum*

OFFSETS
....

Some houseplants produce shoots round the base of the plant called 'offsets'.

Offsets can be carefully removed with a sharp knife when large enough, ensuring they have some roots, and planted into individual pots.

SUITABLE PLANTS

Plants that produce offsets include:

- *Aloe vera*
- *Echeveria*
- *Haworthia*
- Lady palm, *Rhapis excelsa*
- Pink quill, *Tillandsia cyanea*

PLANTLETS

Some houseplants conveniently produce
plantlets at the end of their long flowering stems.

Wait for the leaves and
roots to form before
severing them from the
main plant and potting
them on.

PROPAGATION
COULD NOT
BE EASIER.

SUITABLE PLANTS

Plants that produce plantlets
include:

- Spider plant, *Chlorophytum comosum*

- Moth orchid, *Phalaenopsis*

- Creeping saxifrage, *Saxifraga stolonifera*

Cape primrose *Streptocarpus*

These popular houseplants are grown for their showy, colourful flowers that appear over several months. Choose a variety with colours to suit your taste or interior design. They are easy to propagate from leaf cuttings, so you can have an endless supply to give to friends and family.

Growing

Starter plants are best purchased in pots from garden centres or online. They can remain in that pot for a year or so but will then need potting on into fresh compost and possibly into something larger if they have outgrown their pot. Keep them on an east- or west-facing windowsill to avoid direct sunlight during summer. During winter and autumn move them to a window with more light (e.g. south facing) if available. They can be grown in the greenhouse but will need shade during the summer months.

Maintenance

Pot up *Streptocarpus* every two years into fresh compost and a larger pot. Use a houseplant or peat-free multi-purpose compost. Feed with a potash liquid every two weeks during spring and summer. Water regularly when the compost feels dry to the touch but avoid over-watering. Remove stalks and flower heads after flowering.

Propagation

Simply cut a young healthy leaf down the midrib and cover this edge with hormone rooting powder. Make a shallow groove in potting compost in a seed tray, place the leaf with the cut edge into it and firm the soil around it. After a few weeks, plantlets will appear that can be removed and potted on individually.

THREE TO TRY

'Crystal Ice' – white flowers with the lower lobes covered with deep blue, fine veins. Flowers over a long period.

'Targa' – velvety, deep blue-purple flowers that appear in loose clusters from spring through to autumn.

'Ruby' – clusters of rich red flowers, up to 6cm (2¼in) across, with mid-green, primrose-like foliage.

Jade plant *Crassula ovata*

Jade plants are tender evergreen succulents with fleshy, rounded green foliage, sometimes edged with pink or red. They are also known as money trees, because according to Chinese proverbs they bring wealth and prosperity. Star-shaped white or pink flowers appear in autumn.

Growing

Usually grown as small to medium in size, jade plants can live for years. Although slow growing, they can reach 1 or 2m (3 or 6½ft) in height and spread if potted on regularly. They are a low-maintenance plant with tolerance of a variety of indoor conditions. They prefer natural light but will tolerate some shade. The edges of their leaves will take on a reddish tinge when exposed to high levels of light.

Maintenance

Grow in cactus compost and feed four times a year with a balanced liquid feed. Water sparingly and just when the compost feels dry to the touch. Remove flowers and stalks when they have started to go over, unless you are collecting their seed. Trim branches to keep the size contained.

Propagation

Propagate by sowing seed or cuttings taken from leaf or stem. Harvest seeds when ripe and sow indoors in a propagator at 15–18°C (59–64°F). For leaf cuttings, remove a leaf and leave the severed end to dry for a few days. Then dip in hormone rooting powder and place the severed section in potting compost. Plantlets will form after a few weeks – remove carefully and pot on individually. For stem cuttings, take an 8cm (3in) length of stem, dry out the wounded section, then place in potting compost.

THREE TO TRY

'Variegata' – variegated foliage featuring distinct green-and-white markings.

'Hummel's Sunset' – grows up to 1m (3ft) in height and width, and has fleshy rounded leaves edged with yellow and red.

'Minima' – dwarf variety with branching stems and fleshy green leaves, sometimes edged with red.

Snake plant *Sansevieria trifasciata*

With attractive fleshy, sword-like upright leaves, these foliage plants make great-looking features. Extremely drought resistant, they are ideal if you are away from home a lot and unable to water regularly. Considered bomb-proof by many, they are good for beginners or those not too confident in their green-fingered abilities.

Growing

Plants need to be kept at above 10°C (50°F) all year round, but apart from that they are tolerant of most conditions. They will cope with both light and shade and humid or dry conditions. Plants can be grown in cactus compost or a 50:50 mix of peat-free multi-purpose compost and horticultural grit (see page 31 on compost types).

Maintenance

Water sparingly when the compost feels dry to the touch. In winter cut watering down to about once every six weeks. Snake plants are fairly slow growing so will not need repotting often, if at all. If it does outgrow its pot, transfer to another that is just a couple of centimetres larger. A mature plant can become top heavy, so you may want a heavy pot to ensure it does not topple over.

Propagation

The easiest way to propagate the snake plant is from leaf cuttings. Remove a healthy leaf and use a sharp knife to cut an upside-down V-shape into the bottom of it. Leave the leaf out to dry for a few days. Then insert the base of the leaf into a jar of water, ensuring the water just covers the inverted V. After a few days you will notice roots growing from the base of the leaf. A couple of weeks later and you will notice baby plants appearing around the base of the inverted V. Leave them to grow bigger and then when they are about 4cm (1 ½in) high they can be carefully removed and potted on individually into a pot with cactus compost.

THREE TO TRY

'Laurentii' – probably the most popular variety due to its striking pale yellow margin running up the lengths of the leaves.

'Black Coral' – intriguing variety with dark-green-and-black mottled foliage and an upright habit.

'Silver Flame' – chunkier sword-shaped leaves than some of the other snake plants, with a pale grey-green band running up the foliage.

CHAPTER 6

PLANTS FROM SUPERMARKET SCRAPS

Supermarkets present a wonderful opportunity to grow plants for free. After the initial purchase of the fruit, vegetable or herb, it is possible to grow plants by either sowing their seed or planting the scrap part. In some cases, it might be possible to get hold of free products if they have passed their 'best before' dates.

In this chapter you will learn which plants to look out for at the supermarket, how to get them started once home and how to look after them when they start growing. There is also information on plants that you can grow from leftover roots and stems as well as those you can grow from seed, such as tomatoes and peppers. For something more exotic, there are tips on how to grow ginger and turmeric. And you will discover how to grow fruit trees for your back garden or patio.

GROWING FROM THE SUPERMARKET

There is a plethora of vegetables, fruits and herbs that can be regrown from food bought from the supermarket. Soon your kitchen windowsill could be full of delicious free food and beautiful-looking plants.

APRICOT

PEACH

PLUM

SPROUTING STALKS AND VEGETABLE TOPS

There are many vegetables that will regrow from scrap vegetables. The most common ones are lettuce, onion, leeks, garlic, spring onions and celery. Simply plant the base of the plant into compost or water and it will regrow some more shoots and leaves. Carrot tops can also be planted to produce delicious fresh foliage that tastes like parsley.

POTATO TUBERS

We have probably all encountered potatoes that we have forgotten about in a cupboard somewhere and discovered a few weeks or months later once they have grown sprouts. Those potatoes, if planted in the ground or compost, will grow into a plant and produce

more tubers underground so that you can keep harvesting them. Sweet potatoes will also regrow from their tubers, and if you have somewhere warm and sheltered in the garden, you can harvest your own if you plant them in spring and cover them with a fleece to protect them from frost.

FRUIT TREES

Most fruit such as apples, pears, plums, peaches and cherries will grow from pips and seeds if planted in compost. Whilst they will not necessarily come true from seed, they can still develop into beautiful trees. If you want something a bit more exotic, try growing an avocado from a stone. Even if it never produces any fruit, it makes a great houseplant.

CARROT TOP

POTATO TUBERS

LEMON GROWN FROM PIP

SPICY ROOTS

Ginger and turmeric are two easy crops to grow from the supermarket. Simply select plump swollen tubers (the roots) and look to see whether they have swollen buds starting to break through the surface. Cut the root into 5cm- (2in-) long sections, ensuring each one has some of these swollen buds. Soak the root in water for about 12 hours then plant the sections individually in pots, placing the tuber just below the surface of the compost. Leave it in a light, warm place but not in direct sunlight. In a few weeks you will see shoots coming out of the tuber. If left, they will develop into attractive houseplants. Alternatively, continue to pot up the ginger into larger pots, and you will have enough to snap off sections of the roots and use them in cooking. Repot the remaining plant and it will continue to grow and produce more tubers for cooking.

HERBS

When you shop at the supermarket for leafy herbs you usually have a choice between buying the leaves or buying the plant. The latter is by far the best option because you can propagate it and have a continual supply on the kitchen shelf. Herb plants worth considering at the shops include mint, basil and rosemary. Although the plant itself will grow on the windowsill for a few weeks, if you take cuttings you can have an endless supply.

To propagate, take a softwood cutting from the herb at about 10cm (4in) long, strip off the lower leaves and place it in a glass of water (see Basil, page 78). Once roots start to emerge, plant in a pot to allow more flavoursome foliage to grow. When you start to get low on stocks, simply take another cutting and start the process again. You may never need to buy herbs from the supermarket again!

GINGER

TURMERIC

BASIL IN WATER

FRUIT AND VEG SEEDS

Many fruit or fruiting vegetables from the supermarket are packed full of seeds. These include tomatoes, peppers, strawberries, melons and pumpkins. This is a win-win situation, because not only do you get to eat the food, but afterwards you can save the seeds and grow crops. You may never have to buy the crop again from the supermarket!

Tomatoes

For a taste of the Mediterranean, there is nothing like fresh tomatoes. They can be grown in pots, bags or directly in the soil, and can be propagated from slices of shop-bought tomatoes.

Sowing

In spring, take a ripe tomato and cut it into slices about 3mm (¹⁄₁₀in) thick. Space them equally on multi-purpose compost in a seed tray, leaving 1cm (½in) between each slice, then cover with another 1cm (½in) of compost. Place in a propagator or on a sunny windowsill.

Growing

After about a week the seedlings will germinate. Prick them out into individual pots when they are about 8cm (3in) tall, and plant them outside once the risk of frost is over. Tomatoes require a sunny, sheltered location either outside or in a greenhouse. They are annuals and so will die at the end of the summer and can then be added to the compost heap. They will need a 2m (6½ft) vertical cane or string to grow on. Pinch out any sub-laterals growing from the leaf axils as they develop, to allow the energy to go into ripening fruit. Once they start to flower, feed once a week with a high-potash liquid feed (usually called tomato feed in garden centres).

Harvesting

Pick fruit as it starts to turn red. Tomatoes that are still green by the end of the season can either be made into delicious green tomato chutney or placed in a drawer with a ripening banana to help turn them red.

Peppers

Whether you prefer fiery hot chillies or milder bell peppers, most supermarket pepper seedlings will reward you with bumper crops of delicious flavoursome fruits from mid- to late summer.

Sowing

Pepper seeds should be sown in mid-spring indoors. With bell peppers choose a red variety as they are the ripest, so the seeds will germinate. With other chillies, there is variation between colours depending on their variety, so choose ones that have matured to a good size and feel nice and firm. Cut open the peppers and inside you will see hundreds of white seeds. Scrape them out and place them on a sheet of kitchen paper to dry out for a few hours. Sprinkle the seeds lightly over a seed tray filled with compost and cover over with another layer of compost about 1cm (½in) thick. Water the plants then place either on a sunny, warm windowsill or in a propagator.

Growing

When the seedlings are about 5cm (2in) high, they can be carefully pricked out into individual pots. Once the risk of frost is over, they can be planted into larger pots and kept in a conservatory or greenhouse, or outside in warmer climes. Water well during dry spells and once flowers start to form they can be given a high-potash liquid feed.

Harvesting

Bell peppers can be picked at different stages of their ripeness, with green being the earliest and most mild, yellow being somewhere in between, and red being the ripest and with the strongest flavour. If you fancy growing them the following year, simply scoop out the seeds and store them until the following spring, when you can repeat the process and sow them again.

Apple tree

Apple trees bought online or from plant nurseries are usually grafted onto rootstocks to restrict their size. Yet naturally they regenerate by germinating from their pips found in the centre of the fruit.

Sowing

Cut open an apple and remove the seeds. There can be as many as six seeds in the centre of the fruit. Choose brown pips, avoiding the unripe white ones. Sow each pip into 9cm (3½in) potting compost and place outside in a sunny location to encourage them to germinate.

Growing

When a seedling reaches 10cm (4in) it can be potted into a larger pot. Keep potting on into larger pots as it outgrows its old one. Unless you have a large garden, apple trees grown from seeds are best grown in large pots to restrict their size. Prune them every winter by removing any crossing branches and to allow sunlight into the canopy. Keep plants in pots watered regularly during the summer and grow them in full sun.

Harvesting

Apple seedlings will probably not come true from seed but will share some of the parent's traits. It will probably take longer to come into fruit production than a grafted tree, but they say good things come to those who wait. Not all trees grown from apple pips will produce fruit, so it is worth growing a few if you have room.

POLLINATOR

APPLE BLOSSOM

PIPS

PIPS

Cantaloupe melon microgreens

Most of us enjoy eating the sweet, succulent fruit of a melon. Collect the seeds and, if you have a greenhouse, you can grow them as plants that may produce fruit. A simpler and quicker way to enjoy melon is to grow its flavourful tiny leaves and shoots.

Propagation

Cut the melon in half and remove the seeds in the centre of the fruit. Run them under a tap in a sieve to remove the stickiness, because they can be slippery and difficult to sow when covered in the melon's pulp. Drain the seeds then sow them over the surface of a seed tray filled with potting compost. Keep the sowing quite dense with only about 3mm (1/10in) between each seed.

Growing

Place the seeds on a sunny windowsill or a propagator if you have one. Keep the compost moist, and in a few days you will start to see shoots emerging. In a couple of weeks the melon seeds will be about 3cm (1in) high with tiny leaves, and these are the microgreen melons.

Harvesting

Use a pair of scissors to trim off the tops of the shoots and the tiny leaves. They taste delicious in salads and smoothies. They will sometimes regenerate and give you a few more flushes of microgreens after the first harvest. Occasionally some leaves can taste bitter, which some people like, but it is simply down to luck and the seeds. Sow a new batch if the taste is not to your liking, as there can be variation in flavour.

NEW CROPS FROM OLD VEG

There are lots of different veggies you can grow easily for free using your supermarket scraps. All you need is a sunny windowsill, a pot, compost and a bit of patience. Within a few weeks you will be harvesting fresh homegrown vegetables without having had to sow a single seed.

Lettuce from scraps

Supermarkets sell a number of different types of lettuce, and they can be used to produce more leaves by planting the base after you have finished with the leaf. The main criteria is they have a stalk where they were originally cut from the ground. Loose leaves in bags cannot be propagated.

Propagation
Save the stalk, being sure it has 2cm (¾in) left of growth above it. Use a sharp knife to tidy up the top of the stalk where the leaves were cut (ensuring you still have about 2cm/¾in left of growth above the stalk). Place the stalk in a shallow bowl of water, 1cm (½in) deep, for 48 hours, to allow the stem to rehydrate.

Growing
Remove the stalk from the water and plant it into a 9cm (3½in) pot filled with compost. The stalk should be just below the soil level, with the 2cm (¾in) of growth just above it. Place the plant on a light and warm windowsill. Alternatively, if it is spring or summer, the lettuce stalk can be planted outside, directly into soil. Lettuce tolerates some light shade but will cope with full sun too. Keep the plant well watered in dry weather.

Harvesting
After a couple of weeks you will notice the leaves starting to grow upwards from the stalk. Harvest leaves with scissors as and when you need them. They should produce a few more flushes of leaves after the first time they are harvested. Once they have finished producing leaves they can be added to the compost heap.

Garlic

Garlic is one of the easiest of all the scraps to grow. Cloves left out in a bowl in the kitchen sprout shoots without even trying – they want to sprout, so you are only facilitating this instinct.

Propagation

Remove individual cloves from the paper cluster of bulbs. Make sure their basal plate (the base at the bottom of the clove) is intact and not damaged. Fill individual 9cm (3½in) pots with multi-purpose compost to just below the top, then push a clove into the centre. The tip should be just below or flush with the surface of the compost.

Growing

Place pots on a sunny windowsill until the tip starts to sprout. At this stage you can either move it outside into a warm sunny spot and plant it directly into the soil, or continue to grow it indoors on a windowsill. Sprouted garlic cloves can be planted out in mid-spring, which will give them the whole summer to form bulbs. They require full sun in fertile, well-drained soil. Avoid heavy, wet soil as this can cause the cloves to rot.

Harvesting

If grown indoors, as an alternative to harvesting the bulb, you could harvest the shooting sprouts. Also known as scapes, they can be added to salads, stir fries and soups as a mild flavouring. Garlic is ready to harvest when the foliage has turned brown and yellow and started to wilt. Bulbs should lift from the compost in the pot by simply turning the pot over and tugging the bulbs with your hands. Bulbs in the ground may put up more resistance, in which case you can use a fork to prise them free. Dry out garlic for a few days before storing. To grow more, repeat the process the following year.

BOTANICAL GLOSSARY

One of the major factors to successfully propagating plants is having a basic understanding of some essential botanical terms. This helps you identify the key anatomy of a plant and grasp processes such as germination and pollination, which are necessary for seeds to be produced and ripen. It will also mean you know which parts of a plant you can take cuttings from.

SEED GERMINATION

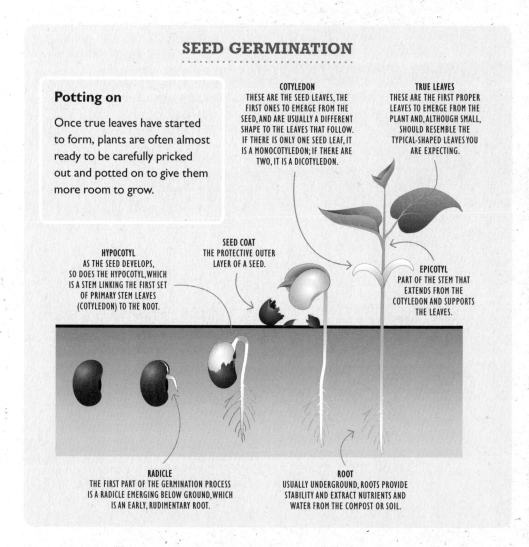

Potting on

Once true leaves have started to form, plants are often almost ready to be carefully pricked out and potted on to give them more room to grow.

COTYLEDON
THESE ARE THE SEED LEAVES, THE FIRST ONES TO EMERGE FROM THE SEED, AND ARE USUALLY A DIFFERENT SHAPE TO THE LEAVES THAT FOLLOW. IF THERE IS ONLY ONE SEED LEAF, IT IS A MONOCOTYLEDON; IF THERE ARE TWO, IT IS A DICOTYLEDON.

TRUE LEAVES
THESE ARE THE FIRST PROPER LEAVES TO EMERGE FROM THE PLANT AND, ALTHOUGH SMALL, SHOULD RESEMBLE THE TYPICAL-SHAPED LEAVES YOU ARE EXPECTING.

HYPOCOTYL
AS THE SEED DEVELOPS, SO DOES THE HYPOCOTYL, WHICH IS A STEM LINKING THE FIRST SET OF PRIMARY STEM LEAVES (COTYLEDON) TO THE ROOT.

SEED COAT
THE PROTECTIVE OUTER LAYER OF A SEED.

EPICOTYL
PART OF THE STEM THAT EXTENDS FROM THE COTYLEDON AND SUPPORTS THE LEAVES.

RADICLE
THE FIRST PART OF THE GERMINATION PROCESS IS A RADICLE EMERGING BELOW GROUND, WHICH IS AN EARLY, RUDIMENTARY ROOT.

ROOT
USUALLY UNDERGROUND, ROOTS PROVIDE STABILITY AND EXTRACT NUTRIENTS AND WATER FROM THE COMPOST OR SOIL.

PARTS OF A PLANT

When propagating plants it is useful to be able to identify their various parts, as this helps when collecting material such as semi-ripe cuttings, buds for grafting or leaf and stem cuttings.

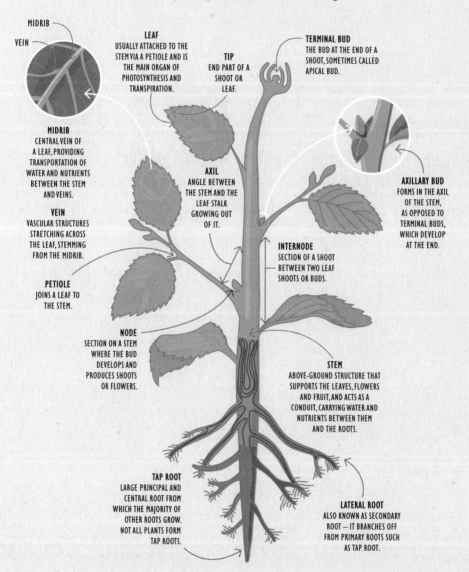

MIDRIB

VEIN

LEAF
USUALLY ATTACHED TO THE STEM VIA A PETIOLE AND IS THE MAIN ORGAN OF PHOTOSYNTHESIS AND TRANSPIRATION.

TIP
END PART OF A SHOOT OR LEAF.

TERMINAL BUD
THE BUD AT THE END OF A SHOOT, SOMETIMES CALLED APICAL BUD.

MIDRIB
CENTRAL VEIN OF A LEAF, PROVIDING TRANSPORTATION OF WATER AND NUTRIENTS BETWEEN THE STEM AND VEINS.

AXIL
ANGLE BETWEEN THE STEM AND THE LEAF STALK GROWING OUT OF IT.

AXILLARY BUD
FORMS IN THE AXIL OF THE STEM, AS OPPOSED TO TERMINAL BUDS, WHICH DEVELOP AT THE END.

VEIN
VASCULAR STRUCTURES STRETCHING ACROSS THE LEAF, STEMMING FROM THE MIDRIB.

INTERNODE
SECTION OF A SHOOT BETWEEN TWO LEAF SHOOTS OR BUDS.

PETIOLE
JOINS A LEAF TO THE STEM.

NODE
SECTION ON A STEM WHERE THE BUD DEVELOPS AND PRODUCES SHOOTS OR FLOWERS.

STEM
ABOVE-GROUND STRUCTURE THAT SUPPORTS THE LEAVES, FLOWERS AND FRUIT, AND ACTS AS A CONDUIT, CARRYING WATER AND NUTRIENTS BETWEEN THEM AND THE ROOTS.

TAP ROOT
LARGE PRINCIPAL AND CENTRAL ROOT FROM WHICH THE MAJORITY OF OTHER ROOTS GROW. NOT ALL PLANTS FORM TAP ROOTS.

LATERAL ROOT
ALSO KNOWN AS SECONDARY ROOT — IT BRANCHES OFF FROM PRIMARY ROOTS SUCH AS TAP ROOT.

THE ANATOMY OF A FLOWER

For a flower to produce fertile seed it needs to be pollinated. Here are some terms that explain the various parts of a flowering plant that make pollination possible.

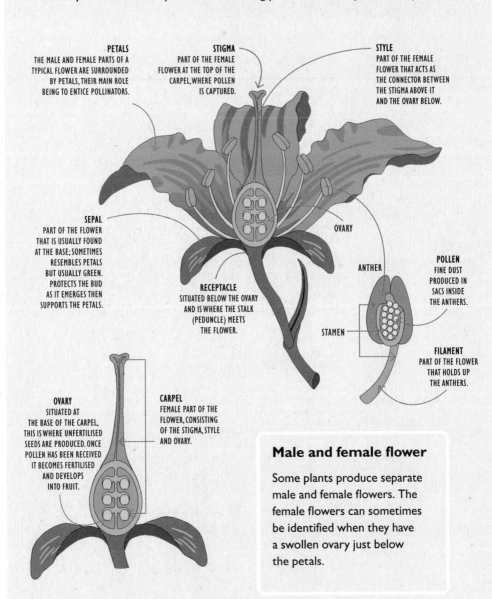

PETALS
THE MALE AND FEMALE PARTS OF A TYPICAL FLOWER ARE SURROUNDED BY PETALS, THEIR MAIN ROLE BEING TO ENTICE POLLINATORS.

STIGMA
PART OF THE FEMALE FLOWER AT THE TOP OF THE CARPEL, WHERE POLLEN IS CAPTURED.

STYLE
PART OF THE FEMALE FLOWER THAT ACTS AS THE CONNECTOR BETWEEN THE STIGMA ABOVE IT AND THE OVARY BELOW.

SEPAL
PART OF THE FLOWER THAT IS USUALLY FOUND AT THE BASE; SOMETIMES RESEMBLES PETALS BUT USUALLY GREEN. PROTECTS THE BUD AS IT EMERGES THEN SUPPORTS THE PETALS.

OVARY

RECEPTACLE
SITUATED BELOW THE OVARY AND IS WHERE THE STALK (PEDUNCLE) MEETS THE FLOWER.

ANTHER

POLLEN
FINE DUST PRODUCED IN SACS INSIDE THE ANTHERS.

STAMEN

FILAMENT
PART OF THE FLOWER THAT HOLDS UP THE ANTHERS.

OVARY
SITUATED AT THE BASE OF THE CARPEL, THIS IS WHERE UNFERTILISED SEEDS ARE PRODUCED. ONCE POLLEN HAS BEEN RECEIVED IT BECOMES FERTILISED AND DEVELOPS INTO FRUIT.

CARPEL
FEMALE PART OF THE FLOWER, CONSISTING OF THE STIGMA, STYLE AND OVARY.

Male and female flower

Some plants produce separate male and female flowers. The female flowers can sometimes be identified when they have a swollen ovary just below the petals.

PROPAGATION GLOSSARY

Some of the terminology used in propagating plants can seem a bit dauting to start with. However, they quickly become easy to use and understand.

DEADHEADING

Abscission
The separation or detachment of two parts of plant material. Usually refers to deciduous leaves naturally dropping from trees in autumn.

Annual
A plant that germinates, flowers and sets seed all within a year. Sometimes bedding or tender plants are referred to as annual because they will not survive the winter, even if in warmer climates they would be perennial and continue growing for another season.

Apical dominance
Most plants grow from the leading or terminal bud of a plant, which dominates the growth habit and inhibits other lateral or side branches.

Biennial
A plant with a two-year life cycle, within which time it will germinate, flower, produce seed and die.

Breaking bud
When a plant awakens from dormancy and a bud starts to open, breaking through its protective bud scale.

Bulbil
A small bulb formed in the axil of a leaf, which can be a useful method of vegetative propagation. Alternatively, a bulblet is a smaller bulb growing from another bulb.

Deadheading
Removing the old flower head after flowering to encourage more flowers later. If you do this the flower head will not produce ripe seed, although subsequent ones should.

Deciduous
A plant that drops its leaves in winter, or when the temperature gets cold.

Dormant
When plants are not actively growing. With most plants this happens when the temperature lowers during winter.

Ericaceous

Describes acidic soil with low pH, or below 7pH (neutral), suitable for growing plants such as blueberries, rhododendrons and camellias. The word is derived from Erica, a type of heather.

Evergreen

A plant that retains its leaves all year round. Not all evergreen plants are 'green' though and can be various other colours, including variegated foliage.

Feathered maiden

A one-year-old tree with branches; often refers to fruit trees. A tree without any branches is known as a 'maiden whip'.

Foliage

Another word for leaves; can include deciduous and evergreen leaves, as well as pine needles.

Germinate

When seeds break their dormancy and start to grow. The usual requirements for germination are warmth, sunlight and water.

Hardy

A plant that can be grown outside all year round and is tough enough to withstand frosts and cold weather.

Herbaceous

Non-woody stems of a plant such as those found on annuals and herbaceous perennials (young herbaceous stems of shrubs and trees turn into woody growth).

Mother plant

Sometimes known as a parent or donor plant, it is the plant that a cutting or seed is collected from. Parent is more often used for seed collection when there has been cross-pollination of a male and female plant.

Perennial

A plant that survives for several years. This can include trees, shrubs, herbaceous plants and succulents.

Potting on

Moving a plant to a larger container when it has outgrown its current one.

Pricked out

When seeds are established in pots, seed trays or modules, they are removed carefully from their original sowing position and either placed into a larger pot or directly into open ground.

HERBACEOUS
PERENNIAL

MOTHER PLANT

Seedling

A young or small plant that has not reached full maturity and has been grown from a seed, not from a cutting.

Shrub

Both trees and shrubs are woody perennial plants but generally the term shrub is used to describe a plant that is smaller than a tree and multi-stemmed.

Rootball

Usually refers to the system of roots attached to a plant and its accompanying soil, whether it is being taken out of a container or dug out of the ground.

Tree

Can be both evergreen or deciduous; usually single stemmed and grows taller than a shrub.

Rootstock

Some plants are grafted onto the roots of another plant because the root has either better resistance to pests and disease or because it restricts the height of the plant.

Scion

The stem section of a desired plant that is grafted onto a rootstock.

Seed drill

A shallow row made in the soil where seeds are sown.

SEEDLINGS

RESOURCES

Books

RHS 50 Ways to Start a Garden:
Ideas and inspiration for growing
indoors and out
Simon Akeroyd
(Mitchell Beazley, 2022)

RHS You Will Be Able to Garden
By the End of This Book
Simon Akeroyd
(Mitchell Beazley, 2023)

RHS Practical House Plant Book:
Choose the best, display creatively,
nurture and care, 175 plant profiles
Zia Allaway, Fran Bailey
(DK, 2018)

RHS How to Grow Plants from Seeds:
Sowing seeds for flowers, vegetables,
herbs and more
Sophie Collins, Melissa Mabbitt
(Mitchell Beazley, 2021)

RHS The Little Book of Cacti & Succulents:
The complete guide to choosing, growing
and displaying
Sophie Collins
(Mitchell Beazley, 2022)

RHS Plants from Pips: Pots of plants
for the whole family to enjoy
Holly Farrell
(Mitchell Beazley, 2015)

The Little Book for Plant Parents:
Simple tips to help you grow your
own urban jungle
Felicity Hart
(Summersdale, 2021)

Grow Your Own Garden:
How to propagate all your own plants
Carol Klein, Jonathan Buckley
(BBC Books, 2010)

RHS The Little Book of Small-Space Gardening:
Easy-grow ideas for balconies, window boxes &
other outdoor areas
Kay Maguire
(Mitchell Beazley, 2018)

RHS Complete Gardener's Manual:
The one-stop guide to plan, sow, plant
and grow your garden
Royal Horticultural Society
(DK, 2022)

RHS Handbook: Propagation Techniques:
Simple techniques for 1000 garden plants
Royal Horticultural Society
(Mitchell Beazley, 2013)

Websites

rhs.org.uk
The Royal Horticultural Society. Extensive
gardening information and advice; Plant
Selector searchable database; campaigns
such as Greening Grey Britain to help with
alternatives to paved front gardens; Plants
for Pollinators list.

www.tiktok.com/@
simonakeroydgardener
Gardening video advice by Simon
Akeroyd, including how to grow
plants from food scraps.

INDEX

ACKNOWLEDGEMENTS

I would like to thank Sorrel Wood, Caroline Elliker and Katie Crous from Quarto for their wonderful help and support when writing this book. Also a big thank you to Robin Pridy for her editing skills.

Thanks to Simon Maughan from the Royal Horticultural Society for his advice and comments. Thanks to Jane Lanaway for design, and John Woodcock for the beautiful illustrations.

CREDITS